"I am tired of vacuous elegies and reductive, Red State prognoses that assume there is something rancid or hopeless about places that are hard to find on a map. Such accounts leave little to no room for queering lives and possibilities. That is why I am so thankful that trans activist and scholar Z. Zane McNeill brought together fifteen scholars, artists, and activists to share their nuanced, vibrant take on all things Appalachian and queer. Readers will appreciate the honest, raw call-outs of racism, gendered violence, and environmental injustices that simultaneously reclaim indigeneity, Blackness, non-binary genders, and queerness as local in origin and equipped to build new queer archives that push and gather us together. This collection is a must-read for activists and scholars seeking a fuller sense of queerness as a political enterprise always becoming and undone, shaped by an insistence that y'all matter—I can hardly think of a more pressing project for our times."
—Mary L. Gray, 2020 MacArthur Fellow, author and editor of dozens of articles and several books, including *In Your Face: Stories from the Lives of Queer Youth* and *Out in the Country: Youth, Media, and Queer Visibility in Rural America*

"These deeply personal and theoretically informed essays explore the fight for social justice and inclusivity in Appalachia through the intersections of environmental action, LGBTQIA+ representational politics, anti-racism, and movements for disability justice. This Appalachia is inhabited by a queer temporality and geography, where gardening lore teaches us that seeds dance into plants in their own time, not according to a straightedged neoliberal discipline."
—Rebecca Scott, author of *Removing Mountains: Extracting Nature and Identity in the Appalachian Coalfields*

"Weaving together stories of intersectional queer life with questions of place, politics, and belonging, *Y'all Means All: The Emerging Voices Queering Appalachia* offers readers a nuanced and necessary portrait of Appalachia. These essays are as raw and vulnerable as they are smart and context-driven, each one offering richer understanding of the region through powerful personal testimony. A much-needed remedy to the reactionary views of Appalachia we get from mainstream presses and corporate news, this book is balm."
—Raechel Anne Jolie, author of *Rust Belt Femme*

T0035642

"This collection adds important voices to the chorus rising from the region, singing their own songs and telling their own stories. Playing with genre, form, subject, and positionality, the text offers a beautifully messy vision of a beautifully messy place. The resistance to category serves us all, pushing boundaries and reminding us of the superficialities of most boundaries that shape us. The inclusion of voices unused to existing in the same volumes—of gerontologists and artists and farmers and activists and folklorists and more—creates an overwhelming sense of complexity. That complexity is precisely what we need in mind when we try to write about Appalachia, or when we try to write about queerness. This collection is disruptive and unsettling—in the very best ways. Just when we think we understand queerness in Appalachia, it is troubled and turned inside out again, leaving us uncertain and inspired to keep asking questions."

—Meredith McCarroll, author of *Unwhite: Appalachia, Race, and Film* and coeditor of *Appalachian Reckoning: A Region Responds to Hillbilly Elegy*

"This exuberant collection tears away falsehoods, challenges hierarchies, and presents memoir and scholarship on new ways of understanding the Queer past and present of Appalachia. Resisting conformity, hatred, and oppression in Appalachia is to resist these nationwide. These writers demonstrate not only that Appalachia is central to LGBTQIA+ activism, but also that queerness in Appalachia is central to the wider movements for dignity, equity, and social justice in the United States."

—Steven Stoll, author of *Ramp Hollow: The Ordeal of Appalachia*

"Too often writers and artists from Appalachia find themselves on the defensive, responding to the many ways that popular media misrepresents the region and erases complexities of gender, race, and sexuality. Not so in *Y'all Means All: The Emerging Voices Queering Appalachia.* As members of radical queer communities, the authors imagine the past, present, and future in Appalachia with sharp analysis and glorious storytelling. They define Appalachia on their own terms, with theoretical ferment, honesty, and heart."

—Jessica Wilkerson, associate professor and Stuart and Joyce Robbins Distinguished Chair in History, West Virginia University

"Appalachia is often painted with a broad stroke of a dominant narrative. *Y'all Means All: The Emerging Voices Queering Appalachia* has reworked this narrative to show these hollers ain't all the same. This collection is here to amplify the queer voices and stories bouncing off of the mountains to bring them onto the page. Overlooked and overshadowed by the dominant narrative, this collection works to reconnect queerness with the region through signposts of identities, marginalization, and trauma. It's complicated, for sure, but this collection shows how stereotypes of the region are not only about image but can do real damage. Because families, identities, roots, language, history, and policy are so marred in the past and running deep in the roots of the region, these essays feature a more rhizomatic approach to these cultural concepts. In 'Crafting Queer Histories of Technology,' Hannah Conways says, 'There are always many ways to tell a story, to tell a history.' This collection works to do just that."
—Tijah Bumgarner, filmmaker

"The works in *Y'all Means All: The Emerging Voices Queering Appalachia* are thoughtful, well-researched, emotionally resonant, and beautifully made, all of which balances their sometimes harrowing imagery, and the hard truths they must share about queer experiences in a region that has not always treated the LGBTQIA+ community with the care it deserves. Z. Zane McNeill has done a service for the public good in bringing together the eclectic perspectives of artists and makers from across a broad field of scholars, creative writers, photographers, naturalists, and more. I was continually moved by the love I felt expressed for Appalachia in this collection, a love soldered and made stronger by pain and resilience, by healing and kindness. I really cannot imagine an open-hearted reader not returning that feeling of love toward this book, built as it is on hope, generosity, and the recognition that every voice belongs in the chorus."
—Jesse Graves, professor of English and Poet in
Residence, East Tennessee State University

"This collection provides another space for queer-Appalachian storytelling and analysis. The chapters address Appalachian queer and racial activism, archival histories, and other queer histories including crip/queer theories and histories. Many of these chapters use personal narratives to drive home their points. Several use academic theories to demonstrate the complexities of Appalachian queerness and how this scholarship fits within the academy. This collection is powerful and full of good intentions. We need loud voices such as these to empower those who may be afraid or unable to speak out. Tennessee Jones quotes Jayne Anne Phillips, who says 'This Ain't the South.... It's the goddamn past'; however, this collection shows that Appalachia has an incredibly bright and powerful queer future."

—Travis Rountree, assistant professor of
English, Western Carolina University

"An Appalachian kaleidoscope of queer voices, *Y'all Means All: The Emerging Voices Queering Appalachia* is a varietal collection of authors who explore and complicate how identities can be multifaceted in the mountains. Ranging from Appalachian grassroots organizations who advocate on the behalf of the mountains through artists working against queer stereotypes in the region to religious intersectionality and more, these voices yell out: 'Appalachia is queer too!' This collection of essays is timely and necessary considering the current political, and even economic, climate in Appalachia. It may be the case that these writers, artists, and activist are speaking truth to power in many instances. It is refreshing, nevertheless, to see so many queer-Appalachians forging a diverse future of Appalachia that demands inclusion."

—Caleb Pendygraft, PhD, assistant professor of
Humanities, Massachusetts Maritime Academy

Y'all Means All

The Emerging Voices Queering Appalachia

Edited by Z. Zane McNeill

ISBN: 978–1–62963–914–7 (paperback)
ISBN: 978–1–62963–925–3 (ebook)
Library of Congress Control Number: 2021936592

Cover design by John Yates/www.stealworks.com
Interior design by briandesign

10 9 8 7 6 5 4 3 2 1

PM Press
PO Box 23912
Oakland, CA 94623
www.pmpress.org

Printed in the USA

Contents

Acknowledgments

I was recently interviewed by author Tennessee Jones and assistant professor Oskar Hazard concerning growing up queer in Appalachia. About halfway through the interview, Tennessee paused and said, "We usually ask folks what Appalachian means to them, but it seems to me like you are the first person who would say Appalachia itself is queerness." I smiled and replied, quoting an interview conducted by *Country Queer's* Rachel Garringer, in which Kenny Bilbrey says, "I feel like a part of being Appalachian is inevitably queer—whether or not you identify as queer. I think just the whole experience is."[1]

I grew up in Morgantown, West Virginia, but didn't consider myself Appalachian until I was in graduate school. It was during this process of seeing myself as Appalachian that I also began to identify as queer. About this time, Queer Appalachia's *Electric Dirt* was released. That was the first time I really saw a queerness that spoke to me—it was the first time I really felt *seen*. #dirtqueer #ruralresistance #cornbreadcommunism #appalachianrevolt. I liked the way these words rolled off of my tongue. It felt like coming home.

After reconciling with these two aspects of my identity, I created an Appalachian activist, academic, and artistic community to celebrate queer and trans life in the hollers and hills that I named @marxinthemountains. It was through this community that I was able to facilitate this collection. This anthology is a testament to queer love, grit, and solidarity. I am extremely thankful for the remarkably varied contributors that have given voice to both the frustrations and furious devotion we have to our region. I want to thank the tree sitters, the dancers, the archivists, the writers and poets, and the teachers for imagining and fighting for our Appalachia.

I would also like to give special thanks to those who have mentored me during this process and helped unveil the complexities and gatekeeping of academia and publishing—Travis Stimeling, Hannah Conway, Jessica Cory, Beck Banks, and Matthew Sparks. It is only with your help that I was able to create this platform to raise the voices of those of us who have been historically marginalized.

In solidarity,
Z. Zane McNeill

NOTE

1   Rachel Garringer, *The Republic of Fabulachia: Queer Visions for a Post-Coal Appalachian Future* (PhD diss., University of North Carolina, 2017), 10, accessed October 8, 2021, https://cdr.lib.unc.edu/concern/dissertations/c534fp36b.

Introduction

Z. Zane McNeill

> With under-documented cultures and communities, there is often a gatekeeper...we get to define our Appalachia with our own images and truths...through sharing tales of wildcrafting our queerness, foraging for pieces of ourselves within the intersections of coal mines and class, race and religion, food justice and colonialism.
>
> —*Electric Dirt*[1]

Queer Appalachia's 2017 zine *Electric Dirt* archived the voices of queer-Appalachian language, identity, and community. Armed with terms like "dirt femme," "granny witch," "fag hillbilly," "plant queer," and "gay redneck," a new generation of Appalachian queer artists, activists, and emerging scholars have decided to reclaim "Appalachia" as an inherently queer space. Born and raised in West Virginia, I felt marked as "Other" when outside of the region. "You're from Appalachia? But you sound so smart!" "Did you grow up mudding and eating deer jerky?" "Were your parents cousins?" The more I've considered what makes me queer, the more I have questioned if Appalachia itself is a *queered* place—a region rendered deviant through the lenses of the opioid crisis, poverty, and environmental degradation.

Until recently, the Appalachian region has been eclipsed by an interest in the American Midwest and South in rural Queer Studies. As recently as 2016, scholars Mary Gray, Colin Johnson, and Brian Gilley's keystone work *Queering the Countryside* imagined the "rural" as a space best exemplified by chapters exploring rural Canada, the American Midwest, and the South. Gray, Johnson, and Gilley contend that the "rural" is often perceived as deviant, backward, and invariably *queer*. Similarly, Appalachia, a space containing around twenty-five million people, or around 8 percent of the US population, is a strange and contested space in the American imagination. It stretches through thirteen states, following the Appalachian mountain range from New York to Alabama and is coded both ideologically and politically as "out of place."[2] Appalachia is more than a geographic region—it is an environmental space with a history of natural resource extraction; a cultural construction fashioned by conservatives and liberals to support revisionist arguments of what "America" is, and which bodies represent "America"; and a politically contested space that pushes disadvantaged voices to the margins. Queerness in Appalachia is, therefore, not only in dialogue with rural conceptions of sexuality and gender but also with place-making and spatial politics.

Appalachian culture surged in academic and popular interest with the 2016 release of *Hillbilly Elegy* by venture capitalist cum author J.D. Vance, who will once again be in the spotlight surrounding the forthcoming film adaptation. Vance's memoir explores the moral failings and inherent wrongdoings of poor "Scots-Irish" folk in Appalachia and the Rust Belt. Growing up poor in Ohio and ending up on a huge book tour as a Yale Law School grad, Vance speaks of having to abandon his upbringing to thrive. This portrayal of Appalachia is inherently politicized; it blames the economic pressure that Appalachia faces not on the region being ravaged by extractive industries but on an almost genetic, essentialized failing of its inhabitants. Vance's book actively ignores the roles of capitalism, monopolies, and corporations in devastating Appalachia, never touches on his Appalachia existing because of the colonization of Indigenous lands, and ignores the lived experience of nonwhite folks who call the mountains home.

Public historian Elizabeth Catte, in her 2018 book *What You Are Getting Wrong about Appalachia*, explains that Appalachia is "a political construction, a vast geographic region, and a spot that occupies an unparalleled place in our cultural imagination."[3] She herself is hesitant to term a universalized concept of Appalachian identity and usually works with those who self-identify as Appalachian instead; historically speaking, who counted as "Appalachian" was decided by those in power or with massive amounts of capital. The construct of what and who is Appalachian is inherently a political project that builds on stereotypes of the region. Author Leah Hampton has recently written that:

> These assumptions and disturbing associations have been socially constructed, and they live deep in our national psyche. Americans

have always used rural spaces to validate and perpetuate toxic masculinity, erase people of color, and justify destroying ecosystems.[4]

Henry Caudill's 1962 book *Night Comes to the Cumberlands* described Appalachia as "depressingly defeatist" and Appalachians as a people of the past.[5] Sociologist Rebecca Scott explains that "representations of the Appalachian region . . . suggest *a place* forgotten by time."[6] Sociologist Dwight Billings contends that not only has contemporary Appalachia been perceived as "backward and homogenous" (the standard perception of the region since the 1960s) but also as "right-wing and racist" by liberals across the United States in the wake of the 2016 American presidential election.[7] In this "media-constructed mythological realm," Appalachia is again cast as an "Other."[8] In *Transforming Places: Lessons from Appalachia* (2012), academics Stephen L. Fischer and Barbara Ellen Smith described Appalachian "Other-ness" as:

> Framed within the cultural politics of nationhood, Appalachian is an internal "Other," a repository of either backwardness and igno-rance, or, alternatively, the homespun relics of the frontier; in both cases, it is a place behind the times, against which national progress, enlightenment and modernization can be measured.[9]

Sociologist Jack Weller, in *Yesterday's People: Life In Contemporary Appalachia*, describes his time in West Virginia as feeling like being "stran-gers in our own country, among a people who did not seem to understand us and whom we did not understand."[10] He goes on to say that "the great-est challenge of Appalachia, and the most difficult, is its people," who he describes as lazy, exotic, and "separate" from the rest of America.[11] Though Weller is writing about "Mountaineer culture," he is really writ-ing about how Appalachia is not like "the rest" of America, and, therefore, about what America is, because of what is it not. The myriad of voices in the 2019 collection *Appalachian Reckoning* illustrate that this "Othering" of Appalachia is still a contemporary issue, with the success of *Hillbilly Elegy* and the "rediscovering" of Appalachia, a "forgotten tribe," after the 2016 election.[12]

If Appalachia is seen as culturally backward,[13] so much so that it has been considered "America's unique 'other,'"[14] then I argue that Appalachia would be the inferior of the America/Appalachia dualism.[15] Wouldn't this nonnormative "America" then be able to be considered *queer*? Even more than that, is queer itself a "spatial" term?[16] If Appalachia is a place "out of line" of the normative, then Sara Ahmed argues that this "disorients the picture and even unseats the body," meaning that Appalachia as a queer place inherently queers Appalachian bodies.[17] The perception of Appalachia as culturally "toxic" essentially positions both the region itself and the people who live there as queer.

Y'all Means All moves past the recent reactionary trend in writing on Appalachian Studies, instead centering marginalized voices in explaining how they understand themselves as simultaneously queer and Appalachian individuals. This act of self-definition is extremely important in queer-Appalachian communities, which have been historically written out of metronormative LGBTQIA+ and other Appalachian histories. As Appalachian educator Adam Denney has written, "Make no mistake: erasure is an act of violence."[18] By naming ourselves and our queerness, we create a queer counterpolitics that can reimagine Appalachia as queerly oriented.[19] "As narratives are claimed and reclaimed, we create spaces identifying with multiple aspects of self."[20] This means that through queer storytelling, those who identify as queer and Appalachian can create their own narratives to explain what queerness in Appalachia looks like. English scholar Amanda Hayes has written that "stories are the best ways I know to make people real, to make them human."[21] This necessity of creating queer media and archiving queer-Appalachian worlds is an obstinate theme in this collection.

In their 2020 collection *Storytelling in Queer Appalachia: Imagining and Writing the Unspeakable Other*, scholars Hillery Glasby, Sherry Gradin, and Rachael Ryerson contend that "Appalachian queerness remains underrepresented, misunderstood, sometimes muted and sometimes invisible."[22] Multiple collections recently have fought to make queerness in Appalachia "visible [and] viable"—to challenge normative portrayals of Appalachia and the rural as a cishet space.[23] These anthologies— such as *Walk Till the Dogs Get Mean: Meditations on the Forbidden from Contemporary Appalachia* (2015), *Queering the Countryside: New Frontiers in Rural Queer Studies* (2016), *Electric Dirt* (2017), *What You Are Getting Wrong about Appalachia* (2018), *LGBTQIA+ Fiction and Poetry from Appalachia* (2019), *Appalachian Reckoning: A Region Responds to Hillbilly Elegy* (2019), *Bible Belt Queers* (2020), and *Storytelling in Queer Appalachia* (2020)—have invited writers, poets, activists, artists, and academics to explore, imagine, and describe *their* Appalachia. This Appalachia is a diverse, multifaceted, and often contradictory space in which queer not *only* survives but thrives. For many of us, self-definition of Appalachia is in and of itself activism: by reclaiming what it means to be "Appalachian," we imagine a place of resilience in which *y'all* really means *all*.

It is through this "self-definition" that a negotiation of what it means to be queer and Appalachian is conducted. Communications scholar Mark Hain has argued that it is through the act of "'talking back' to the dominant culture" and participating in queer worldmaking by "engagement with memory and history" that rural queers have created their own identity and self-purpose.[24] Through the act of story-sharing we create a communal history of queerness in the rural, as well as a definition of queerness in Appalachia.[25] As theologist Justin Ray Dutton has written, "telling one's story of being queer and Appalachian represents an important aspect of naming and claiming one's place."[26] This act of naming is extremely important—how can we create an Appalachia that not only includes but also centers voices that were historically written out of the narrative of what it means to be Appalachian? Composition professor Lydia McDermott has argued that "projects and renamings such as [Affrilachia and Fabulachian] echo Appalachia but subvert dominant narratives of time and space and identity in Appalachia, causing a productive disorientation."[27] By naming ourselves and our places through queer lenses, we are asking: What would/does a *queer* Appalachia look like?

In exploring Appalachia as an inherently queer space, we also become entangled with structural violence. "I want to queer my space and my time; I want to hillbilly," contends McDermott. Despite the idealism embedded in our writing, we also reckon with issues within our own communities, such as structural white supremacy, pink capitalism, settler colonialism, and homonationalism. If Appalachia has the potential to be a revolutionary queer space, what are the implications of this for Indigenous populations? What about the continuing violence faced by Affrilachians and Latinx Appalachians? How do we imagine a queer Appalachia that isn't ours to begin with? Filmmaker and scholar Tijah Bumgarner has contended that "stories make claims on the space and those who occupy it."[28] In which ways are uplifting queer-Appalachian voices a settler project in and of itself? Is queer storytelling an act of occupation? However, it is through these political projects that we are able to "counteract objectifying histories" that write out marginalized Appalachian histories.[29]

The first section of this collection, "Finding Self and Discovering Queer in Appalachia" invites contributors to reckon with the tension between their queer and Appalachian identities. These narratives touch on the importance of naming oneself and one's region and coming home to (or with) a queer-Appalachian identity. In "Trans Appalachian: An Interdisciplinary Exploration," media scholar Beck Banks introduces this collection by exploring the cyclical nature of media attention on Appalachia and the queer and trans embodiment in Appalachia, as well as the queerness of Appalachian time and space. Photographer Julie Rae Powers focuses on the multiplicity of selves that we have as queer folks in Appalachia—this complex, muddy, and stubborn love for our roots, community, and mountains—in "Queer in the Holler: Appalachian Image Making." Writer Tennessee Jones's chapter, "How I Got My Name," is a contemplation on the process of change, of finding and refinding identity and reforming the self. These chapters illustrate the amazing and freeing possibilities of being, living, and thriving as queer in Appalachia and touch upon the tension and grief of loving a place and its people while not *being at home* there.

Pieces in this section also voice the frustration of being written out of "who counts" as "Appalachian" and the tendency of Northern liberals to write off Appalachia and the South as "beyond repair," despite the amount of important organizing being done in the region concerning queerness, racial justice, woman's rights, and immigration. In social work graduate student e.k. hoffman's chapter, "Different Creatures," hoffman argues that to write off the South is to ignore the work of queer and trans Black, Brown, Indigenous, and People of Color (BBIPOC), to disregard the violence being faced by over half of the Black population in the US, and to abandon our most marginalized communities at a time when their existence is ever more precarious under an increasingly authoritarian regime. Likewise, in "For Black Appalachians, Southerners, and Rural Folks," Afro-Appalachian activist M.AMA explores the ongoing policing of tone, identity, and embodiment she faces in both progressive spaces in the North and queer-Appalachian spaces. These narratives compellingly illustrate the entanglements many queer-Appalachians face between sexuality, regional identity, religion, race, and self-representation.

Questions of tone—What voices are "Appalachian"? What is the *right* way to say "Appalachia"? What accent is *allowed* to be queer?—are represented in the artist sair goetz's chapter, "All Them That Don't Call Me

They." One aspect of self-definition is to hear your voice and experience reflected as *authentic*. So many of us lose our voice—our accents—or code switch in non-Appalachian spaces in order to be recognized as competent; reading Foucault out loud in my Appalachian tongue in graduate school was not an option. If I wanted to be seen as an authority, my "redneck" accent had to be buried. Thus *speaking* Appalachian is inherently a political project. In "Appalachian Accent and Academic Power," a chapter in *Appalachian Reckoning*, rhetorician Meredith McCarroll explains that by refinding and reclaiming her voice and identity—as queer and as Appalachian—she was able to find home in the "disparate layers" of selfhood. By speaking Appalachian as an academic, she believes that "the voices of the past will not be lost, but can find a way to go on and on and on."[30] goetz's chapter is contextualized by this—the power of speaking their identity with their "home tongue" is inexorably an activist project. By voicing nonbinary as "nawn-bai-nare-re," goetz is creating a space where identity is performed as queer/Appalachian and imagining a future space in the region that would reflect that home embodied by that language of queerness.

The second section of the collection, "Queer Hills, Hollers, and Mountain People," invites activists, artists, and scholars to theorize a queer-Appalachian framework that engages with Appalachian queer histories, contemporary queer ecologies, queer temporalities, queer embodiment(s) of Appalachian protest, and the role of queer of color critique in Appalachian activisms. From a queer history of the AIDS epidemic in Johnson City, Tennessee, explored by journalist Samantha Allen in "Your Own Country," to a political reading of contemporary queer Black activism by poet and scholar-activist Heather Brydie Harris in "Homegrown," these pieces emphasize that Appalachia and the South are brimming with queer histories of resistance informing contemporary queer life and community organization today. It is through doing the work of finding and contextualizing these queer histories that the potential to create a queer-Appalachian futurity is born.

Aaron Guest's chapter "Rainbow Aging: Negotiating Queer Identities among Aging Central Appalachians" challenges the conception of LGBTQIA+ life in Appalachia as a relatively new phenomenon. Guest raises the voices of LGBTQIA+ Appalachian elders who have had to conceal their identities or face the dual challenges of heterosexism and rurality. This chapter illustrates that navigating queer identities in

Appalachia is something LGBTQIA+ folks have done for an extremely long time. Queer Appalachia/Appalachians is not new—it is just that only recently have we been able to document and archive our experiences, raise our community's voices, and challenge the metronormative focus of LGBTQIA+ studies.

In "An Appalachian Crip/Queer Environmental Engagement" and "Plant Time" critical disability scholar Rebecca-Eli Long and critical dance scholar Kendall Loyer explore the interconnections between the body/embodiment and one's environment/place-making practices. While Long engages and comments on the historic extraction and exploitation currently disabling Appalachia, Loyer reimagines seed-saving as an action of solidarity and resilience. Both of these authors use their chapters as a way to reckon with contemporary issues in Appalachia (rooted in neoliberal capitalism) to point us toward potential queer futures. By engaging with assemblages and more-than-human actors, such as Loyer's "Microcosm," we are able to actively perform resistance and establish a queer-Appalachian praxis.

These critiques against extraction, settler colonialism, and exploitation are met head on in activist Chessie Oak's piece "Tree Sit Blockades and Queer Liberation." As an integral part of the campaign and movement Appalachians Against Pipelines, Oak's piece weaves together a history of resistance in Appalachia that continues to fuel contemporary grassroots campaigns. They explore the political importance of the body enacting a blockade as a tool to disrupt the continual abuse caused by capitalism and colonial heteropatriarchy. In their narrative, they describe queerness as a tool for Appalachian world-making based on dismantling oppressive hierarchies and violent power structures.

The last section, "Creating the Queer-Appalachian Archive," invites scholar-activists to engage with the need for queer storytelling, myths, icons, and images, as well as to explain the importance of creating, finding, and engaging with queer-Appalachian histories and archives. In "Myths and Electricity," Maxwell Cloe explores the metronormative skew in Queer Studies that has historically eclipsed LGBTQIA+ Appalachian voices. This absence in the academic archive has led to a DIY style of archive creation that queer-Appalachians have taken upon themselves to create and maintain. The most well-known, and controversial, example being Queer Appalachia's zine *Electric Dirt*, as well as its corresponding digital archive and Instagram community, which Cloe analyzes thoroughly. This focus on queer representation and place-creation is also reflected in linguistic anthropologist Brent Watts's piece, "The Man, the Moth, the Legend." In this chapter, Watts analyzes the Mothman, a popular Appalachian cryptid, as a queer-Appalachian icon and a meaning-making practice conducted by the queer community in Appalachia. In Watts's analysis, he turns to the representations of the Mothman by artists shared on Queer Appalachia's Instagram account to illustrate the use of speculative fabulation in queering folklore and assembling creative queer-Appalachian futures.

Though Watts and Cloe describe Queer Appalachia's account as constructing a narrative of Appalachia that is antifascist, queer, and oriented around harm reduction and mutual aid, in 2020 the *Washington Post* published an exposé alleging potential grifting and money-laundering practices. In response, the queer Black-Appalachian community voiced grievances concerning tokenization, erasure, appropriation, and cultural theft. Queer Appalachia's defensive response, described by many as gaslighting, alienated many in the community and led to a deep discussion concerning white supremacy in queer spaces, the use of trans Black voices as proof of "wokeness," and the harm enacted by white queer activists toward BBIPOC in both Appalachian spaces and those beyond the mountains.

Mamone, of Queer Appalachia, and Sarah Meng wrote in their chapter for *Storytelling in Queer Appalachia* that "[they] dream of a day when reparations are taken seriously, not just racially but through a lens of corporations and capitalism also."[31] However, the *Washington Post* piece alleging financial misconduct by Queer Appalachia challenged whether or not Queer Appalachia's actions aligned with this discourse. In "Lessons for the Long Term," DiaspoRican and zinemaker Rachel Casiano Hernandez explores the more widespread trouble with majority white organizations in activist spaces, where white leaders often benefit from settler colonialism and harm communities of color.

Chapters by trained activist-historians Matthew Sparks and Hannah Conway concern the need of creating, discovering, and writing queer history. In Sparks's "The 'Wyrd' and Wonderful Queerness of Appalachian Oral History," he argues that "wyrd" oral history methodologies have the ability create queer-Appalachian worlds, reconcile Appalachian and queer identities, and aid in the imagining of queer-Appalachian futures. Conway's chapter, "Crafting Queer Histories of Technology," investigates the craft of queer identity-making, the violent act of erasure concerning queer histories and Indigenous scholarship, and the power of story-making in challenging the hegemonic power structures propagated by narratives that eclipse LGBTQIA+ lives in Appalachia. Through the exploration of the Tennessee Valley Authority collection as a form of public memory creation, Conway unpacks how narratives of the Appalachian region and its people were constructed and how they affect the collective remembering of Appalachian histories.

Y'all Means All does not seek to define Appalachia, or even queerness in Appalachia. Instead, we provide a platform to uplift the voices of an extremely varied and diverse community who define Appalachia and nonmetronormative queerness for themselves. This collection is born out of optimism—we situate ourselves within an Appalachian history of resistance and envision an Appalachian queerness fueled by radical community-making, mutual aid, and solidarity in movements for intersecting justices. As theologist delfin bautista has written, "Despite some of the hardships experienced in Appalachian areas, there are also many transgressive dynamics of resilience that reflect a long history of queerness."[32] While many have written Appalachia off as a backward and unredeemable place, by doing so they ignore the labor of hundreds, if not thousands, of activists, artists, and scholars who have fought and are continuing to fight for a radical and progressive Appalachia. These are our stories.

NOTES

1   Queer Appalachia, *Electric Dirt*, vol. 1 (Bluefield, WV: Queer Appalachia, 2017), 4.

2   Mary L. Gray, Colin R. Johnson, and Brian Joseph Gilley, *Queering the Countryside: New Frontiers in Rural Queer Studies* (New York: New York University Press, 2016), 15.

3   Elizabeth Catte, *What You Are Getting Wrong about Appalachia* (Cleveland: Belt Publishing, 2018), 10.

4   Leah Hampton, "Lost in a (Mis)Gendered Appalachia," Guernica, November 25, 2020, accessed October 5, 2021, https://www.guernicamag.com/lost-in-a-misgendered-appalachia.

5   Henry Caudill, *Night Comes to the Cumberlands* (Boston: Little, Brown and Co, 1962), 392.

6   *Removing Mountains: Extracting Nature and Identity in the Appalachian Coalfields* (Minneapolis: University of Minnesota Press, 2010), 33.

7   Dwight Billings, "Once Upon a Time in 'Trumpalachia,'" in *Appalachian Reckoning: Region Responds to Hillbilly Elegy*, edited by Anthony Harkins and Meredith McCarroll (Morgantown: West Virginia University Press, 2019), 51.

8   Ibid.

9   Stephen L. Fisher and Barbara Ellen Smith, *Transforming Places: Lessons from Appalachia* (Urbana: University of Illinois Press, 2012), 2.

10   Jack E. Weller, *Yesterday's People: Life in Contemporary Appalachia* (Lexington: University Press of Kentucky, 1965), 2.

11   Ibid., 7.

12   Juana Summers and Jeff Simon, "Why America's White Working Class Feels Left Behind," CNN, September 20, 2016, accessed October 5, 2021, https://tinyurl.com/v2y9at4u; story by Summers, video by Simon.

13   Not only stuck in a queer time and place, as J. Halberstram might explore, i.e., stuck in a mythological past while existing in the cotemporary world, but also perceived as racially and ethnically different than other white people, as argued by T.R.C. Hutton in *Appalachian Reckoning*.

14   Harkins and Meredith McCarroll, *Appalachian Reckoning*, 50.

15   America being perceived as white, heterosexual, patriarchal, and based on Enlightenment rationality.

16   Sara Ahmed, *Queer Phenomenology: Orientations, Objects, Others* (Durham, NC: Duke University Press, 2006), 67.

17   Ibid.

18   Adam Denney, "A Drowning in the Foothills", in *Storytelling in Queer Appalachia: Imagining and Writing the Unspeakable Other*, edited by Hillery Glasby, Sherrie L. Gradin, and Rachael Ryerson (Morgantown: West Virginia University Press, 2020), 66.

19   Lydia McDermott, "Appalachia as a Moveable Space," in ibid., 114.

20   delfin bautista, " Queering Trauma and Resilience, Appalachian Style!" in ibid., 160.

21   Amanda Hayes, "A Letter to Appalachia," in ibid., 33.

22   Glasby, Gradin, Ryerson, ibid., 1.

23   Ibid., 1.

24   Mark Hain, "We Are Here for You," in *Queering the Countryside: New Frontiers in Rural Queer Studies*, 166.

25   Katherine Schweighofer, "'Rethinking the Closet,'" in ibid., 227–28.

26   Justin Ray Dutton, "Challenging Dominant Christianity's Queerphobic Rhetoric," in *Storytelling in Queer Appalachia*, 51.

27   Lydia McDermott, "Appalachia as a Moveable Space"," in ibid.

28   Tijah Bumgarner, "Queering the Appalachian Narrative," in ibid. 173.

29   Rachel Wise, "Loving to Fool with Things," in *Appalachian Reckoning: Region Responds to Hillbilly Elegy*, edited by Anthony Harkins and Meredith McCarroll (Morgantown: West Virginia University Press, 2019), 346.

30   Meredith McCarroll, "Appalachian Accent and Academic Power," in ibid., 253.

31   Gina Mamone and Sarah E. Meng, "Queer Appalachia: A Homespun Praxis of Rural Resistance in Appalachian Media," in *Storytelling in Queer Appalachia*, 212.

32   delfin bautista, "Queering Trauma and Resilience, Appalachian Style!" in ibid., 159.

ABOUT THE AUTHOR

Z. Zane McNeill, the editor of this collection, is an independent scholar-activist from West Virginia. He currently sits on the steering committee for the Appalachian Studies Association and has written on choreopolitics, socially engaged art, critical animal studies, and queer ecologies. They are coeditor of *Queer and Trans Voices: Achieving Liberation Through Consistent Anti-Oppression.*

SECTION 1

Finding Self and Discovering Queer in Appalachia

Trans Appalachian: An Interdisciplinary Exploration

Beck Banks

Since the late 1800s, Appalachia has existed in a constant state of being "rediscovered" within American culture. During these cycles of rediscovery, ideas about Appalachian people, their bodies, and the region's displacement in time emerge. As I began to think about transgender studies and Appalachian Studies in tandem and how they encompass my identity, the overlapping patterns and surrounding dialogue became increasingly apparent. While we can celebrate the rising queer voices of Appalachia, the time is ripe to address specifically the transness of Appalachia. Trans Appalachia speaks to these themes surrounding the body, media attention, and experience of time (aka temporalities). It aims to create space for trans people in Appalachia, at least intellectually, with hopes of more.

Media Attention: Appalachia

As I write this, it is November 2020. The film adaptation of the memoir *Hillbilly Elegy: A Family and Culture in Crisis* premieres on Netflix this month. The book proved to be a phenomenon, spending over seventy weeks on the *New York Times* bestsellers' list. The sales of the book coincided with the lead-up to the 2016 elections. As was stated by the press, Trump's win was due to "Trump Country," an election nickname for Central Appalachia.[1] The region experienced one of its resurgences in the American cultural and media landscape.

The author of *Elegy*, J.D. Vance, never lived in Appalachia, nor did his parents.[2] His grandparents resided in Eastern Kentucky until their teens. Vance makes an outsider claim to the region, writing a pulled-up-by-the-bootstraps memoir about escaping Appalachia's inherited violence and poverty. It's gross and exploitive and profoundly in line with the Appalachian stereotypes.

Rollback to the 1960s, with Lyndon B. Johnson's War on Poverty, Appalachia was as prominent in the news as it was on prime-time television programming that focused on Appalachia. *The Beverly Hillbillies* was one of the decade's top-rated shows, with *The Andy Griffith Show*, *The Waltons*, and *Hee Haw* not far behind. Tangentially related shows like the rural-set *Green Acres* and *Lassie* performed well too. As American Studies scholar George Lipitz noted, there was a nostalgia for rural life as the US began to become increasingly urbanized.[3] The capturing of these cultures on the small screen is referred to as an imperialistic measure.[4] This was one more way to claim territory in the US and tame a land too often portrayed as wild. The focus, as can be seen in the aforementioned examples, was quite white as well.

While the civil rights movement was gaining momentum, it was simply racist that television focused on poor white people, as historian Anthony Harkins points out.[5] It was a way to erase Black people and the nation's role in their marginalization. The same can be said for the War Against Poverty, which focused on Appalachia instead of places with higher numbers of Black people. That isn't to dismiss the people of color in Appalachia; though those stories are rarely told. As Appalachian Studies scholar Elizabeth Catte points out,[6] Appalachian people of color are erased time and time again. When the coal-mining industry was booming, she found that, depending on the place, the mines employed between 20 to 50 percent Black men. The influx of Mexican and South American immigrants to the region in the 2000s never makes the Appalachian narrative either. These are not stories that get told when the media speaks of Appalachia.

Instead, television's "hillbilly" portrayals were often childlike and white, as Media Studies scholar Horace Newcomb pointed out.[7] *The Beverly Hillbillies'* Clampett family never adapted to their home of Beverly Hills. They wore ragged clothes, cooked the same opossum food as before, and cracked Confederacy jokes in their mansion. They were perceived as not deserving their money, because they didn't know what to do with it. While Andy Griffith was not childlike—because he's a sheriff—side characters like Gomer Pyle and Barney Miller were. These tropes exist within hillbilly portrayals as one more way to show their difference. Newcomb notes a binary in this representation; Appalachia is the "Other." People outside of it can feel better about themselves, because they aren't from there. That same trope resurfaced in the 2016 Trump election, when the region was dubbed "Trump Country" in news coverage. It is similar to travel magazine writing about the region in the late 1800s: it objectified; it saw another kind of human. Speaking of which, transgender people have experienced this treatment too.

Media Attention: Transgender

In 2014, Laverne Cox graced *Time* magazine's cover in an issue dubbed "The Transgender Tipping Point."[8] The magazine itself is often cited as a tipping point in transgender recognition too, at least in contemporary times. It should go without saying: transgender people have always existed. Much like Appalachia, trans people also get rediscovered in the press. They have a history of being over-medicalized and two-dimensional. This reductive portrayal echoes the portrayal of Appalachia.

Within American mass media and international news, Christine Jorgensen made headlines in the 1950s after seeking a medical transition in Denmark. She spent the rest of her career speaking on late-night shows and doing the lecture circuit. Tennis star Renee Richards made news for petitioning and getting to play women's tennis in the 1970s. Stories about transgender people appear for a while and float back out of the American consciousness.[9]

If not for Caitlyn Jenner, perhaps attention to transgender issues would have waned among the public. In 2015, Jenner came out as transgender in an article with a front-page picture in *Vanity Fair*. This public relations tactic made major waves. Laverne Cox and Janet Mock—prominent trans women of color and activists—were eclipsed. More attention was paid to Jenner by the mainstream press for a considerable amount of time.

While there are benefits to trans visibility, there is a trap within it. With it, violence toward transwomen of color has increased. Jenner, whose politics are in line with MAGA, proved to be a trans spokesperson for cisgender people only (those whose gender aligns with assigned sex at birth). I might also ask what venture capitalist and memoirist J.D. Vance did for Appalachia. Both Jenner and Vance purported to represent a group of people but did little to nothing to benefit those populations. Profiteers exist everywhere.

The Body

Catte's polemic *What You Are Getting Wrong about Appalachia* links J.D. Vance and Henry Caudill to eugenics proponents.[10] Caudill and Vance are key bestselling authors associated with Appalachia. Henry Caudill wrote about Appalachia in his 1960s book *Night Comes to the Cumberlands*. While Caudill tried to get people in Eastern Kentucky sterilized, Vance's ideology and relationships line up with eugenics. Both appear aligned with this concept of breeding people, a dangerous idea that seeps into Appalachian narratives. Stereotypes seem to posit Appalachian people as products of cousinly love, deeply inbred, riddled with health issues, and, well, responsible for their own poverty. Systemic problems aren't acknowledged. Eugenics is.

The idea of wrong bodies, lesser bodies, appears throughout transgender studies. Some people consider trans people to be derived from medical treatment alone and to be freaks. These ideas are explored in trans scholarship, be it Susan Stryker's use of Frankenstein's monster to illustrate trans rage or Sara Ahmed's social hammers that tell the body what it needs to be.[11] The lesser-body idea can be applied in Appalachian, race, disability, queer, trans, and class-oriented studies. All of this can be brought together to explore marginalized identities. This flawed-body concept extends to other areas, such as the concept of the wrong time and place.

Process/Ritual/Time

Appalachia is often referred to as out of step with time. It is considered backward, existing in the past. These thoughts sound like a queering of temporality. Time relations could be different instead of out of sync with the surrounding world. Trans is sometimes perceived as a throwback to the binary or as too radical for the present; either approach pushes transness and Appalachia out of the present. This displacement is one more power play. Screen studies can help illuminate how different processes of time and communication influence Appalachian and transgender portrayals.

Horace Newcomb says that Appalachia's nature is at odds with that of the television industry.[12] By classic television standards, a good producer makes a show that gets advertisers, a concept that can be updated to include subscriptions now. Newcomb pulls from communication theorist James Carey's conception of transmission/transactional and ritual communication to explain how television needs to be more ritualistic in its program design.[13] To make representation better, the media industry would benefit from viewing programming and storytelling as a process.

While I'm not advocating the trans representation on *Grey's Anatomy*, the series did work with GLAAD to develop a transgender plotline. This approach displaces the rush for time and money, shifting it to a mildly ritualized production approach.

Television and news outlets would also do well to see trans and Appalachia as process-oriented, not just transactional objects. Instead, both are too often steeped in binaries, placing those people in stark contrast to others in society. I wonder if mainstream media can capture the ritualized communication in understanding our marginalized identities, be it in collective, ritual-oriented cultures or journeys of self-understanding. Instead, groups like the Instagram account and zine creator Queer Appalachia, the multi-media group Transilient, the arts and media hub Appalshop, and more take (or took) the responsibility of approaching these more nuanced stories.

There are other issues at play too. Trans people often struggle to get jobs. Appalachia does face an economic disadvantage. These populations encounter problems with getting their stories told, or even imagining telling them; poverty creates a focus on survival. The overlapping of these identities seemingly would face more problems, even more so with race and ability. These complexities present one more reason to explore the intersection of these disciplines and identities: to understand the unique challenges transgender people in Appalachia face, encourage empathy and work toward positive change. If Appalachia can embrace its transness, its queerness, that would send an immensely powerful message to the rest of the country. Perhaps, they are the ones who need to understand what's happening now.

Conclusion

Trans (and queer) and Appalachia seem like a contradiction to most, which is a prime reason why it should be explored. This "contradiction" means people have yet to wrap their minds around this world and the ideas that could be found within these merging identities. Hopefully, the concepts presented above serve as a launching ground to take off from, to evolve. There is room for a lot more work.

In looking at Appalachian Studies and trans studies together, the ideas in political scientist Cathy J. Cohen's piece "Punks, Bulldaggers, and Welfare Queens: The Radical Potential of Queer Politics?" come to mind.[14] Expanding the conversation to include people who feel marginalized in society and at different places in the system allows for the alignment and, thus, empowerment of a group. It opens a discussion that should make systems of oppression accountable.

NOTES

1   While there are many examples of "Trump Country" in the press, the following are a couple of notable pieces: Larissa MacFarquhar, "In the Heart of Trump Country," *New Yorker*, October 10, 2016, accessed October 8, 2021, https://www.newyorker.com/magazine/2016/10/10/in-the-heart-of-trump-country. Lisa Lerer, "Once a Clinton Stronghold, Appalachia Now Trump Country," PBS, May 3, 2016, October 8, 2021, https://www.pbs.org/newshour/nation/once-a-clinton-stronghold-appalachia-now-trump-country.

2   J.D. Vance, *Hillbilly Elegy: A Memoir of a Family and Culture in Crisis* (New York: Harper, 2016).

3   George Lipsitz, *Time Passages: Collective Memory and American Popular Culture* (Minneapolis: University of Minnesota Press, 1997).

4   Ibid.; Anthony Harkins, *Hillbilly: A Cultural History of an American Icon* (New York: Oxford University Press, 2003); Horace Newcomb, "Appalachia on Television: Region as Symbol in American Popular Culture," *Appalachian Journal* 7, nos. 1–2 (Autumn–Winter 1979–1980): 155–64.

5   Harkins, *Hillbilly*.

6   Elizabeth Catte, *What You Are Getting Wrong about Appalachia* (Cleveland: Belt Publishing, 2018).

7   Newcomb, "Appalachia on Television, 155–64.

8   Katy Steinmetz, "The Transgender Tipping Point," *Time*, May 2014, accessed October 8, 2021, https://time.com/135480/transgender-tipping-point.

9   Reina Gossett, Eric A. Stanley, and Johanna Burton, *Trap Door: Trans Cultural Production and the Politics of Visibility* (Cambridge, MA: MIT Press, 2017).

10 Catte, *What You Are Getting Wrong about Appalachia*.

11 Susan Stryker, "My Words to Victor Frankenstein: Above the Village of Chamounix—Performing Transgender Rage," *Kvinder, Køn and Forskning* no. 3–4 (2011): 83–96; Sara Ahmed, "An Affinity of Hammers," *Transgender Studies Quarterly* 3, no. 1–2 (May 2016): 22–34.

12 Newcomb, "Appalachia on Television," 155–64.

13 James Carey, *Communication as Culture: Essays on Media and Society*, rev. ed. (New York: Routledge, 2008 [1992]).

14 Cathy J. Cohen, "Punks, Bulldaggers, and Welfare Queens: The Radical Potential of Queer Politics?" *GLQ* 3, no. 4 (May 1997): 437–65, accessed October 12, 2021, https://tinyurl.com/fjdacnux.

ABOUT THE AUTHOR

Beck Banks is a Media Studies doctoral candidate at the University of Oregon who specializes in transgender media and transgender/queer rurality. They partner with media activist outfits, such as Transilient and Queer Appalachia, to support and research the work these trans-driven organizations do in Central Appalachia. Originally from East Tennessee, Beck is curious about how rural-based trans media activists understand and work within their communities, as well as how they are received by them. To boot, they examine trans television representation and activist efforts—or the performance of those. Having spent years as a reporter and in higher education communication, Beck teaches various courses under the communication and Media Studies umbrella, including public speaking, production survey, and women and Gender Studies.

Queer in the Holler: Appalachian Image-Making

Julie Rae Powers

In the fall of my senior year of undergrad, while engaged to a sweet, amazing boy, I started to have feelings for a tall, slender, gorgeous redheaded girl. This was the start of my coming out journey, which was quite tumultuous. During this time of self-discovery and self-loathing, my dad figured out that something wasn't right. He could read my attraction for said girl like a book the moment I walked into the room with her. This didn't sit well with him. He is a semi-burly, God-fearing mountain man who grew up in the deep hollers of coal country. He was a leader of a church youth group into his late teens, before booze became an intimate pastime, and has recently reconnected with Christianity. My dad and I had a lot of conversations around my sexuality—him or her, right or wrong, "It's a sin," "I love you but," and "I stand by ya anyhow." While the statements were intended to be supportive, I could feel that they were conditional. This made me feel like I had to be straight in order to be loved.

My dad was born across the river from where I was, but we still grew up in the same hollers. When I was around eight my parents moved us to Virginia so that my dad could work for Norfolk and Southern. It was a difficult choice, because we would be leaving behind the majority of our family and a space we knew and were comfortable with, and it was tough for me, because I didn't know what to expect moving to a new state at such a young age. I had spent the years before this swimming in the nearby lake, riding four-wheelers at my uncle's cabin in Ritchie County, playing basketball, and drumming away in a marching band. In this culture, this landscape, I had very limited knowledge of what a gay person was, what they looked like, what it meant. The media had not represented people from where I grew up in a kind way, and there was this implication that you could not be queer and Southern. Donna Jo Smith, a scholar in the

School of Public Health at Georgia State University, provided my first context to why I felt this was true in an essay about the construction of queer and Southern identities:

> The terms *southern* and *queer* both come laden with a host of stereotypes, which we have all internalized to one degree or another. When combined, these stereotypes tend to conflict or conflate, depending on perspective. For some, the notion of a "southern queer" is an oxymoron, conjuring up images of a drag queen with a pickup truck and gun rack or of a dyke with big hair and Birkenstocks. For others, the term *southern queer* is redundant: Since the South is already an aberration, what is a southern queer but deviance multiplied?[1]

While Smith primarily references the South, I very much believe this also applies to Appalachia.[2] My cultural grooming told me that queerness didn't exist where I lived, and if it did, it was surely an abomination. This was the early 2000s when the internet was popular but certainly not what it is now. Myspace was a primary mode of youthful socialization, and Facebook was still limited to college students. Occasionally, I would end up in some random Yahoo or AOL chatroom, but I never had an inclination to search for "gay" peers. The gayest thing I was googling at the time was the Seattle Storm's point guard, Sue Bird, whom I was obsessed with.[3] There was very little queer content on TV at the time, and, if there had been, my mother was censoring a lot of what I watched, so accessing it would have had an extra layer of difficulty.

I think one of the most important women loving women representations I first saw and loved was Callie Torres and Arizona Robins on *Grey's Anatomy*.[4] Their first date happens within the first five or six episodes of season five, which I have rewatched more times than I can count. *The L Word* was on air around this time, but I didn't have Showtime and didn't even know it existed.[5] Other than that, there were a few "gay" people in my very large high school of 2,500 students. One guy was a redheaded theater kid that everyone seemed to love and accept, because he was, in their minds, the palatable stereotype. One girl, who I became very fast friends with (of course), stated very proudly that she was bisexual, which I was too naive to comprehend. Other than that, the only other gay person I had regular contact with was a gentleman with a deep Southern accent (deeper than in the area I resided in) who repurposed the gas

Untitled, Reveal Self, circa 2011

station down the road from my house as a consignment shop. I often went there to kill time. My dad would say, "Oh, you're going down there to hang out with gay Clay!" and would sometimes add in the limp wrist motion.[6]

For the first several months of this coming out journey, I really didn't know what I was. I had kept this from nearly everyone in my life, except my dad; it really wasn't something I volunteered to him but was asked rather point-blank about. I did not have a sounding board, and I fearfully assumed any of my closest friends or family would judge me for it. I carried a very heavy load alone. I felt aspects of shame, like I was sick or something was wrong with me. What if I was the pervert my family had said gay people were? I kept imagining the times some of my family members acted out scenes as very flamboyant gay men in the most mocking way. I kept thinking that was how they would think of me. I find it really difficult to describe the back and forth, push and pull internal struggle I had. I remember standing at the sink at my job at the smoothie bar crying involuntarily, digging deep to keep it together. At one point, I was so taxed about choosing between my long-term fiancé and this girl who, like me, was an artist, was smart, and was an exciting new adventure, that I gave up choosing at all. I gave up making a choice, because it had come to the point where I wanted to kill myself rather than

Salt 1 of 28, 2013–2014

choose. I kept my identity to myself for another nine months. My only solace during this time was making photographs about my secret selves as a way of working through it. In hindsight, this was the groundwork for the images I made in grad school.

Part of my inner push to come out publicly, as well as to my deeply religious mother, was that in a few short months I would be moving to Columbus, Ohio, for graduate school. Columbus was a big deal to me. The biggest town I had lived in up until that point was around fifty thousand people, and that was only because there was a college there. When it wasn't in session, it became a rather ghostly scene. I told myself that I wanted to be 100 percent myself when I arrived. I wanted to be gay, Southern, and confident. I came out to my mother in an email, because I was scared shitless of how she would react. She said she received the email, but she and I didn't talk about it for nearly a year.

I started grad school feeling very free and making whatever type of work came to me on a whim. This was encouraged in your first year of grad school—get weird, get outside of your usual. I felt free enough to even make nude images of my girlfriend, because I was desperate for imagery depicting female/female desire.

After some playtime, I started digging into a direction for my thesis work. This is when things began to get messy for me as an artist and as a queer person. I began photographing my family quite often, because they lived a short two-and-half-hour drive from Columbus. Inspired by the Looking at Appalachia project started by Roger May, I wanted to convey positive or nuanced imagery of Appalachian life with the same motivation that I was sure Roger did. The Looking at Appalachia project was so important to me because it showed people like me, from West Virginia, who were more than just the characterization portrayed by the media. I was able to see real Appalachians with real lives, complex and vibrant. It gave me a sense of pride about being from Appalachia, instead of the typical shame or embarrassment I had carried during my childhood.

I had experienced plenty of prejudice from Northerners, Midwesterners, coastal elites, and even other Southerners for being from West Virginia and for having a thick accent. My younger self had nixed the accent years ago to avoid hearing ignorant shit from people. I didn't want people to perceive me as stupid. Now, I wish I still had it. The sticky part about taking on this endeavor was that both my family and I, together and separately, were working to accept the gay thing. I was still wildly uncomfortable with myself, and I felt very much on the outside of things. I was concerned that I wasn't Appalachian enough to do this project, I was too queer to be part of my family anymore, maybe my family didn't get why I chose art as a profession, and I must be some liberal from the city.

As I photographed my father's home and the life around his ridge more frequently, I could see the direction of my work getting muddied— and so was my purpose in making photographs. I started getting tough questions from my peers and my advising faculty. I had no answers for

Portrait of Pops, 2014

Mom ashing a cigarette, 2015

anyone, not even myself. Then, the most profound question came from a faculty member I admired in a one-on-one studio visit. She asked, "Julie Rae, why did you pick up a camera to begin with?" She saw my confusion and continued, "Why the medium of photography? Why not painting? Or printmaking? Or anything else?" I hesitated, wide-eyed. She said, "The

Michelle and me, 2016

answer is because you never saw yourself. Anywhere. Not where you grew up, not in the media. Photography is your answer to that. It is a way to see yourself."

From that moment, my thesis work took shape as a way to show how queerness exists in Appalachian culture. I was a queer from the holler, and I was out to prove that we existed. Although things were complex, being queer and Appalachian was a beautiful pairing and a possibility. I can't really say that the thesis project got any better from that moment. I was still truly contending with my own internalized issues with my identity. It was so important for me to create this media for myself, because no depictions of queer folks in Appalachia really existed on TV or in the archives. I had very little to reference or look up to.

At the end of three years, I closed my MFA with a thesis exhibition titled "Queer in the Holler." I was content with what I presented but not fully satisfied. I always felt like there was something that wasn't reconciled. I let the work lie after my graduation in May 2016. In the fall of 2019, I revisited the work, because I was keen on sending it into a book competition in order to get the work published by a Southern publisher I admired. Come to find out, it wasn't the work that wasn't reconciled; it was me. I was still wrestling with accepting myself exactly as I was. I was trying to bring together my past self and my present self.

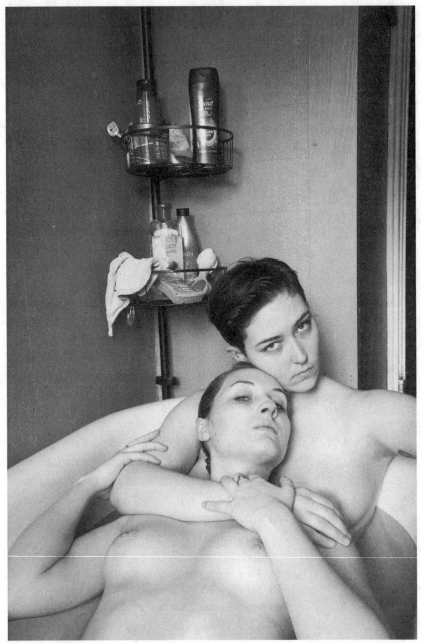

Untitled, Paxton and me, 2016

Ram attacked by wolves, 2016

Many years later, having grown strong, proud, cemented in myself, I realized that the work wasn't just about proving that queer people existed in Appalachia. I made this work as a way of searching, looking, longing, honoring, revering, and accepting my multiplicity of selves. This body of work was a quiet love letter to all the things that created me: the labor of my father and uncles, the sacrifice of the landscape, the grit of my mama and aunts, the comfort of a trailer home, the winding of roads, the thickness of Appalachian humidity, the beauties and pains of my experience, and the mythology of hailing from the mountains. I am queer and I am Appalachian. Photography was the tool that allowed me to accept that there is a multiplicity of selves. I can be a complex amalgamation of Appalachian, Southern, four-wheeler-riding, hunting, tomboy who is a liberal, city-dwelling artist. I no longer have to choose between the past and the present. I get to be complex and nuanced. I get to be all that I am.

NOTES

1   Donna Jo Smith, "Queering the South: Constructions of Southern/Queer Identity," in *Carryin' On in the Lesbian and Gay South*, ed. John Howard (New York: New York University Press, 1998), 370.

2   Some argue that Appalachia is the South, while others believe it is distinctly separate.

3   Sue Bird came out publicly about a decade later.

4   Women loving women has recently been used instead of "lesbians" as a way to be inclusive of transgender individuals, nonbinary folks, bisexuality, pansexuality, etc.

5   I would discover it between undergrad and grad school and watch it secretly in my college bedroom away from the eyes and ears of my roommates.

6   The limp wrist motion became a reductive symbol mocking homosexuality because of the flamboyancy of gay men. Example: "Is he, ya know? *limp wrist motion*."

ABOUT THE AUTHOR

Julie Rae Powers received their MFA in Photography from the Ohio State University and their BFA in Photography from James Madison University. Recently, JR started Soft Lightning Studio, a photography publishing platform dedicated to broadening space in the photo world for image makers who are persons of color, queer, or women, among others. Their work has focused on family history, coal, Appalachia, the queer female gaze, the butch body, and queer chosen families. For their day job, they work as an instructional designer.

Different Creatures

e.k. hoffman

Content Warning: this piece mentions nuclear warfare and subsequent death, imperialism, anti-Semitism, anti-Blackness, childhood abuse, heterosexism, cissexism, and suicide.

I grew up among the Appalachian Mountains in Oak Ridge, a city in East Tennessee that bears the fucked history of being the "Secret City," built as part of the Manhattan Project during World War II. Oak Ridge was a part of the US's imperialist agenda to build the first atomic bomb, a uranium fission bomb called "Little Boy," which was later dropped on the Japanese city of Hiroshima toward the end of World War II. Three days after, the plutonium fission bomb "Fat Man" was dropped on the Japanese city of Nagasaki. The aftermath of both these atomic bombs resulted in the deaths of approximately two hundred thousand Japanese civilians and military personnel. The radiation and nuclear fallout caused generations of health issues. My grandfather was assigned to this top secret project, where he worked on thermal diffusion until the end of World War II, extracting uranium-235, about which he says that he only later realized would become the first atomic bomb.

I learned about Oak Ridge's complicated history growing up, but what the Oak Ridge public school system failed to teach me was that, in actuality, the bomb's effectiveness in ending World War II is largely under debate in the international community, with the ethical implications seriously questioned. Rather, Oak Ridgers tout their "Friendship Bell," which supposedly symbolizes their fraternity with Japan. Cue eye roll. It was this us vs. them mentality in learning about Oak Ridge's role in World War II that I believe contributes to the harmful myth that we must only care about ourselves and those whose similarities are obvious to us, particularly in terms of race and nationality. I still feel the weight of Oak Ridge's history on me today, though I have not lived there since 2013. However, that weight is hard to identify. Is it anger? Or is it guilt? If so, the question is: How do I turn that generational guilt into accountability?

It was Mira Kimmelman, a Holocaust survivor and celebrated memoirist, who cut through some of this noise for me. As my Hebrew school instructor, she encouraged us to research lesser-known Jewish prayers to discuss in class. In this setting, Mrs. Kimmelman recited to us, "*Baruch ata Adonai, Eloheinu melech ha-olam, m'shaneh habriyot*" (Blessed are you, lord, our G-d, king of the universe, who makes creatures different). I found so much power and beauty in this expression of gratitude for uniqueness, as so much of my adolescence, like that of many others, was centered around conformity. Considering myself among the "different creatures" now empowers me both in my role as an organizer and activist and as community member.

I am a disabled, Jewish, Southern, Appalachian, queer, trans, nonbinary activist currently living and learning in Columbia, South Carolina, upon stolen Congaree land. My journey to come into these identities has been an arduous one but also a healing one. Coming out is not a singular event or an experience with a linear trajectory. I come out as all of my identities in varying contexts depending on relevance, but, more so, safety. Particularly, my decision in 2019 to start hormone replacement therapy was both easy and complex. Simple, because I knew I wanted to pursue changes within my earthly form, but difficult, because I questioned what safety would mean socially, emotionally, financially, and, at times, physically, as I sought after medical transition. My intersectioning marginalizations have not been what has made me feel unsafe in certain circumstances but, rather, my fear of the reactions of others to "different creatures," such as myself. But I also want to acknowledge that my experience as a white trans person has granted me the privilege of far more safety than is granted to Black trans folks and other trans people of color.

The personal is political, and my personal experiences with marginalization pushed me into self-advocacy early on. I have long debated with myself what my introduction to advocacy was. Was it when I demanded time in my public elementary school to teach about Jewish customs and history, because I noticed my religious and spiritual culture was not included in the Christian-centric curriculum? Was it when I argued on the playground as a child against using anti-gay slurs? Was it when I fought with my sibling over her use of anti-Black language? Was it when I sought help from a trusted adult outside my family about abuse in the household? Or was it later, more formally, in college, when I started a three-semester social justice program offered by my university's Office of Multicultural Student Affairs? I think all of these instances were entry points to opportunities for advocacy and organizing within my social spheres. However, I think it is primarily important to recognize how we learn and grow in our advocacy, especially as we learn more about communities that are impacted differently than our own. This growth in organizing spaces can come in the form of shedding our egos and halting performative activism.

Performative activism plagues our movement for liberation with folks often doing the work for the clout, recognition, and credit. For example, in my experience, far too many supposed prison abolitionists, usually white, will performatively speak of an end of prisons, but they will still support the presence of school resource officers who perpetuate the school-to-prison pipeline. This stance directly supports the incarceration of Black youth, especially young Black girls, at extraordinarily high rates. This "activism" is a performance; far too often, the ego gets in the way of the work at individual and organizational levels alike. While one could argue that every type of activism is a performance of messaging to apply pressure for a greater good, organizing for the credit is directly opposed to the entire point of organizing: to uplift marginalized voices. The silencing nature of performative activism is violence against those the performer is claiming to serve.

As a survivor of physical, emotional, and social violence, I was once of the mindset that no one would keep me safe besides myself. This belief spurred me to become more involved in advocating for myself and my own identities, but it did not reinforce the necessary thinking or action for collective liberation. Y'ain't free til we're all free, and although we certainly cannot look to the state for protection, we can look to each other. The mantra "Who keeps us safe? We keep us safe!" must be shared without performativity.

For me, an enormous aspect to understanding community empowerment and safety is to acknowledge when power and safety are lacking. Power isn't pie, and what we're fighting for isn't to take a slice from someone else. We have to fight not only for power itself but also for the understanding that power isn't zero-sum. We must also center the concept of self-empowerment, by challenging the concept that power can be granted. Within our collective struggle for liberation, we must leave no one out; *we keep us safe.*

We keep us safe in a society that tries to force us into the margins. My role has often been the privileged journey that many formally educated white queers have: access to paid organizing work. With paid work in LGBTQIA+ advocacy, interpersonal violence prevention, HIV/AIDS outreach, youth coordination, and disability rights, I have found that although these are opportunities can further advocacy work, the most powerful work has been through grassroots organizing here in South Carolina.

Much of the most impactful organizing work done in South Carolina has been done by queer and disabled youth of color. Youth members of several local organizations collaborated on creating protest art targeting the 2016 anti-trans bathroom bill, S.1203, proposed in the South Carolina Senate. The bill, which proposed that all public accommodations be segregated by sex assigned at birth, was put forward by Senator Lee Bright during a wave of anti-trans legislation across the Southeastern United States in Spring 2016. One of the youth, then thirteen-year-old Black, trans, disabled artist and activist Grayson (also known as "Zero") powerfully testified, "Please don't do this to my community and please don't do this to me." The bill was subsequently defeated.

I worked with Zero again later that year. Completing a lot of fun and creative collaborative projects, including putting on the South Carolina Queer Youth Prom, growing a garden as a part of a Queer Eco-Project, and mapping the history of police brutality in the United States, Zero was an integral part of community, particularly as someone facing multiple marginalizations. Personally, he was a brilliant and shining figure in my life who taught me so much about being trans and disabled. Unfortunately, Zero felt that many of the struggles he faced were insurmountable, and just two years after his powerful testimony in the Senate judiciary subcommittee, Zero died by suicide, at the age of fifteen. I feel his loss every day.

Having struggled to accept my own learning and psychiatric disabilities (ADHD, c-PTSD, bipolar disorder, depression, and anxiety), I had lost multiple jobs, experienced houselessness, and attempted suicide twice before Zero's death. Zero's death altered me and my understanding of the work radically. Zero's inability to access help was primarily due to the invalidation that disabled youth, especially Black disabled youth, experience. I learned that it was absolutely essential that how I move in this world must be intersectional, especially along the lines of racial justice, disability justice, and anti-adultism. I name this privilege: I learned through others that intersectionality is a must, not through the experience of its absence.

I share these experiences to convey a message: the South and Appalachia should not be written off as places that are beyond repair, "backward," or ignorant. There are self-empowered organizers who are throwing down to lead and stand in solidarity with people marginalized along the lines of race, ethnicity, class, sex, gender, sexuality, immigration status, language, and disability; we are "different creatures" sharing and creating power through community care and the rejection of toxic individualism.

The South and Appalachia have a unique history shaped by rurality and social, religious, and political conservatism. Marginalized people have long lived in the South and Appalachia, and our diversity has enriched the spaces we occupy tremendously. The resilience of the organizers and activists in the South is to be admired, but, as I once had the privilege of hearing author and activist Brittany Packnett Cunningham say, "Resilience is not a requirement for respect." As we all seek survival during both individual and collective trauma, during ever-increasing state surveillance, during a global pandemic, during economic upheaval and the mistreatment of the working class, I remind myself that survival and resilience are powerful. But survivin' ain't thrivin', and I hold onto hope for a better world through committing to putting in the work. As SONG's former codirector Paulina Helm-Hernandez said, "Are you willing to be transformed in the service of the work?" For me, the answer to that is a resounding "yes." Are you?

ABOUT THE AUTHOR
e.k. hoffman (they/them//ze/hir) is an Appalachian, disabled, trans, queer, Jewish activist currently living and learning in Columbia, South Carolina. Ze completed hir BA in Political Science and Gender Studies in 2017 and is currently pursuing a master's in social work at the University of South Carolina. Hir current focuses in study and activism include challenging capitalism, combating adultism, advocating accessibility, and creating safe and brave spaces for transgender folks, especially youth. e.k. has a passion for serving the South and deep love and respect for the

power of Southern and Appalachian folks in our intersectional fight for liberation. In hir free time, e.k. enjoys rowing, painting, cuddling hir cats, and cooking (in cast iron, of course).

For Black Appalachians, Southerners, and Rural Folks

M.AMA

I am a Black Appalachian. I am a Black Appalachian, because I am a slave-descended Black American, and Southern Appalachia is where a large portion of enslaved Black people originated from. I am a Black Appalachian, because I was born there. Although currently away, a Black Appalachian is all I can ever be.

For too long my identity has been policed. Be it race, gender, ability, or region—if it were up to others' critique, I'd be nothing at all. Owning the Appalachian identity has been an endless battle. The very cultures and aesthetics manipulated into stereotypes that plague white Appalachians and Southerners are ones that I have been barred from and rejected. Too Black for that they say, but my history says something different.

Black American history is of migration. Those with firm roots are the minority among us. Anti-Black laws and actions prevent us from owning too much land or growing too large a population. In my home state, West Virginia, Black folks are four times more likely than the state average to be victimized by police killings. These are mostly in central regions, and I believe that's a large reason that my family settled in a historically Black town in the panhandle. But even there, one can clearly see officers from the hills swarming Black neighborhoods to meet quotas.

Policing doesn't end with the law. Even in more progressive spaces I'm policed. I don't sound Appalachian enough. I don't live deep enough in the state. And, once again, I don't have the generations to prove my claim to the identity. In his 2017 book *The Cooking Gene*, culinary historian Michael W. Twitty paints a South that ebbs and flows with the migration of Black families, spanning from Maryland to Oklahoma. His reasoning can be found in the history behind those migratory paths. Melungeon history shows a similar phenomenon; these Black-Indigenous Appalachians moved as far west as Wyoming, only to return South when they were given the boot. Black history puts the Appalachian identity, the concept of identity itself, to question. White people, even poor, historically have had the privilege of intergenerational land ownership and a right to community that we are still not afforded to this day. That intergenerational claim to place is most often established as a standard of "true" Appalachian heritage, effectively an exclusive Appalachian pedigree. To hold Black people to a standard that was made without their consideration and gauge their right to identify with a place that has not consistently been accessible to them is both unjust and diminishing of a region's diverse history and culture—of how it came to be and how it has changed over time. Thus are Black Appalachians, Southerners, and rural folk obscured from our homes and sacred knowledge about how we as a people came to be.

For me, Appalachia and the South extends from Virginia to Jersey, the path of my family's post-enslavement migration. They made a small community to share resources, and only two generations down did a few individuals, my mother included, move south when it felt safe to do so. Although my family had changed to fit their Northern environment out of necessity, our culture stayed true to its Southern roots. We are, and have always been, Appalachians.

If God is change, Black people are the proof.

Appalachia is for everyone, regardless of your history or how you pronounce its name.

ABOUT THE AUTHOR
M.AMA is an Afro-Appalachian (commonly pronounced LAY-SHIN/CHIN in her region) from the Eastern Panhandle. Her ancestral ties are to what is controversially labeled tri-racial, Afro-Indigenous and white groups from Delmarva, Virginian, slave migrants, and Arab-Sudanese migrants. Her mother was the first in her family to move out of the Delmarva area to West Virginia, as the community her family built for generations proved to be a safe haven for Black people and communities during periods of large-scale, anti-Black violence in the country. In the Eastern Panhandle, they found much love and support within a community of many cultures, similar values, and occasional diversion in theoretical thought. M.AMA has lived outside of Appalachia for nearly seven years. She graduated from college in New York and

spent the past few years traveling and working in China, Japan, and parts of Europe, mostly in environmental and linguistic fields. Appalachia is deeply rooted in her being. But at this point in life, identity and history don't feel like a significant truth or a constant in her existence.

All Them That Don't Call Me They

sair goetz

TRY TO BE SEEN
AS A WORD
MOST PEOPLE
HAVE NOT HEARD

We often text rather than call, and we see each other on social media rather than IRL. We don't hear each other's voices. This silence can be particularly liberating for those of us whose vocal expression pins us to the gender we were assigned at birth.

The internet is the only place my larynx does not betray me.

You don't assume my gender when you read my words off your phone. My gendered voice, as well as my height and center of gravity, make little to no impact in the world of "sound off." This genderlessness is a liberating silence. More affirming to me than knowing good selfie angles.

But the erasure of voice from the space of social media has also erased other traces of my vocal history.

The me who speaks naturally in my Southern accent is separated from the me who found a community of trans folks across the world over the internet. My Southern accent, often unconsciously buried under years of vocal conformity, comes out when I speak with other Southern people. That fact carries fear for me whenever I go back to the South. Often, when this accent comes out of my mouth, my sense of my own complex gender identity is further erased, and all that's left is the voice of a Southern white woman.

I typically only hear the word "nonbinary" in a sort of newscaster generic accent. In fact, until 2017 or so, I had only *read* the word, scrolling online searching for a community and the words to call myself.

When I do speak in public, in performances and lectures, I teach people to say "nonbinary" the way I wish I heard it growing up—the way I would have read it growing up if the term circulated widely in 1990s Southern elementary school systems. I like to imagine a world in which "nonbinary" is native to my accent—a blend of North Carolina urban and Oklahoma prairie. I like to imagine "nonbinary" growing up natural in other places too, living in as many Southern accents as there are genders.

In the Northern and Western urban settings where I speak in public, my Southern accent is rarely heard, even by me. In daily life, I allow no one to hear the "w" sound or see the jaw movement in my "y'awl," though they have mostly embraced the genderless "y'all," for the fear of that flattened "Southern woman" I hear in my head.

When I brave that vision and stand up to teach folks my version of "nonbinary," I do so in hopes that it will force the appropriateness of gender multitudes into their conception of the South. When I practice this alone, I do so with the faith that if I can speak my gender identity into my home tongue, then one day I can do so in my homeland, and it will place the appropriateness of gender multitudes into the South's conception of itself.

Me:
nawn
baiiii
nare
re

Them:
nɑ::n
ba:ə
neəʳ
ræ

Me:
Y'awl don't even know how heart warmin' that was.

ABOUT THE AUTHOR
sair goetz (seəɾ ɡetz) writes instructions that shift problematic realities into speculative fictions. Their work seeks to leverage the weightlessness of language

to complicate, manipulate, and annotate the weighty matters it circumscribes. This speculative language is inscribed back into reality through bodily performance, video, installation, and signage. The works become lines of inquiry that move propositions about pertinent topics (sexual violation, illusions of safety, gender nonbinaries, the future of literacy, and the stability of self-definition) into the specificities of embodiment (the elasticity of a tongue, an industrial scissor lift, buttons on the left side of a shirt, devices for dialogue, and three hundred pounds of ice). sair received their MFA from the Ohio State University in 2017 and their BA in Visual and Media Studies, Arts of the Moving Image, and Documentary Studies from Duke University in 2011. In 2017–2018, sair was awarded the Dedalus Foundation post-MFA fellowship. sair has shown their work nationally and internationally and completed several residencies across the US and UK: Battersea Arts Center, London, England; SPACE, Portland, Maine; ACRE, Stuben, Wisconsin; Little Paper Planes @ Minnesota Street Projects, San Francisco, California; Vermont Studio Center, Johnson, Vermont; Weir Farm, Wilson, Connecticut; Sedona Arts Center, Sedona, Arizona (with the fourfor collective); Elsewhere Museum, Greensboro, North Carolina.

How I Got My Name

Tennessee Jones

[M]y inheritance was particular, specifically limited and limiting;
my birthright was vast, connecting me to all that lives, and to everyone, forever. But one cannot claim the birthright without accepting
the inheritance.

—James Baldwin[1]

When I was twenty -one, I spent two weeks in jail in Philadelphia, as
part of a mass arrest to protest the prison-industrial complex. We were
arrested without our IDs, and with the intention of doing jail solidarity; we
entered the system as Jane Does. During the previous weeks of organizing,
we had all chosen what we called action names to protect our identities.
Among folks who called themselves Home Cookin, Trainwreck, Twinkie,
Fortnight—I was Tennessee, a name chosen because, as the place of my
birth, it seemed it might belong to me—and because, for my entire life,
people had been forgetting my name, and I was tired of being forgotten.

I spent the first three days in jail crammed into a holding cell so over-
crowded that I spent one night trying to sleep with my head underneath
the toilet. I couldn't piss in front of that many people, and so I held it and
gave myself a urinary tract infection. I'd left my parents' house when I
was eighteen, and in these years I lived between the two extremities my
childhood had prepared me for—the terror of whatever might happen
to me and a depth of beauty I would later come to realize had been made
possible by this terror. I was desperate, and this either freed me or gave
me no choice but to follow the thread of my faith; by this, I mean all that
I hoped for. I had nothing tangible to fall back on, save for the flesh of
my own body, and I remember when I was first handcuffed, I no longer
felt afraid of anything.

Eventually, those of us who had not given up our legal names were separated out and moved into the general population. In many ways, I felt immediately at home among these women. Most of those I talked to were there for retaliating against abusive partners, for trying to get themselves out of a bad situation, in one way or the other. That the system was rigged was not an academic revelation but a given. This was not unlike the attitudes of my father and uncles and cousins, who had all been in and out of jail, or the rest of my family, none of whom had ever bothered to vote, because there wasn't anyone worth voting for. One day at lunch, I remembered being taken on a field trip to the county jail when I was in the fifth grade, and how those Appalachian men had been eating similar shitty white bread sandwiches as we were served in the Philly jail. I was conscious too that the segregated and white supremacist culture I was raised in had never intended for me to talk to these women, for the knowledge of their experiences to affect the way I'd live my own life.

My roommate in cellblock C was a young Muslim woman who accepted my reasons for being in jail with droll bemusement. She could see that I was queer and told me about jail dildos—made with maxi pads stuffed into condoms—and about jailhouse weddings between the women, with bedsheets and paper fashioned into veils and trains and flowers. Women fall in love here, she said. One day, she pulled me aside and pointed to someone I took to be a young butch with high cheek bones and corn rows. "You see him," she said, "He goes by he. You ever think you might be like him?"

Transness seemed an almost unsayable thing in 2000, even among the anarchists and punks whom I'd made my sole community, and I had little language then for what the fuck was going on with me. I felt as affronted by my cellmate's kindness as I did when other inmates would yell at me across the lunch tables, "Hey, why you look like a man?" How terrible it is to have people see things about you that you don't want to be seen or can't yet see about yourself. Now, when I look back on this, I see that young woman taking me aside as a moment of grace.

Our lawyers eventually told us the police commissioner had no intention of letting jail solidarity work in Philly, and that if we didn't give up our names, we would be held indefinitely. I gave the court my legal name and said goodbye to the women in cellblock C. Soon after we were released, I became homeless by choice and made my money, when I made it, from selling plasma or doing day labor. My lover and I spent the fall and winter hitchhiking around the country, and during this time, I completely stopped using the name my parents had given me, in favor of the name of the place I knew I was never going back to. I moved to Brooklyn six months before 9/11, and three years later I transitioned and legally changed my name. I dropped my father's surname and took the last name Jones because it is common, unremarkable. I wanted to cut myself off from the place I'd come from.

Everybody has roots, and these roots are not traceable for everyone. My family has been in North Carolina and Tennessee, by way of Virginia, since the 1600s. Growing up, when I asked where we had come from, my father told me that we didn't come from anywhere. When I finally traced my father's genealogy, I felt a kind of sickening terror, because I'd always had the felt sense, when I was growing up, that these were people who had been in one place for too long and whose spirits had grown stagnant within the history that had brought and kept them there. The West Virginian writer Jayne Anne Phillips wrote of Appalachia, "This ain't the South.... It's the goddamn past."[2] I discovered this quote only recently, and it describes exactly how I felt as a young girl, working in my parents' tobacco fields and having the visceral sense that time and history had moved on without us.

At the core of my story of who I am is a rupture. I have continued, all these years, to love the people—my family—whom, with the exception of my mother, I will likely never see again. As I grow older, I become less certain whether they might think I'm subhuman, or if it's the humiliation of their imagined gaze that keeps me from embracing them. When I went home for my father's funeral ten years ago, there was the uncle who turned away in disgust, the cousins who couldn't meet my eyes, and the aunt who took me outside and said, "Honey, what do you want us to call you now?" I find this contradiction still too painful to hold—my uncle's rejection and my aunt's gentle recognition that I had become so "Other" that she had no name for it. She did the "right" thing, but it is the reality of the conditions that made her question necessary that made it impossible for me to stay there.

For the past twenty years, my friend Oskar, one of the only other Appalachian transsexuals I've been close with, has helped to remind me that all of the things that happened to us did, in fact, happen. A couple years ago, after fucking up an interview for a job I was qualified for, I called him and asked if he ever felt like an imposter.

"Shit," he said. "How could we *not* feel like imposters? I mean, Tennessee, what story do we even have that's ours? We don't have our names. We don't have our gender. We don't have a narrative. We had to trade all of that in so that we could live. Of course, you feel like an imposter."

At the center of my grief, I think, is still the confusion of whether or not I didn't have a choice but to sever my roots and the understanding that I would have been dead a long time ago if I'd not done this. This is what I mean when I say I've followed the thread of my faith toward all that I've hoped for. I feel now that my life is at least half over, and there is a grief of this that arises from the flesh that has something to do with how long it's taken me to understand anything about where I started from. I have started to wonder if what lies on the other side of love is sorrow, if the one is necessary and constitutive of the other.

I want to tell you now of a memory I have from my first year in New York, just after the towers fell, and just before the endless wars started. I was living then with one of the protestors I'd met in jail, and we were in the East Village, it was raining, and we were leaning shoulder to shoulder as we pissed between two cars. We'd been going to anti-war meetings and feeling broken by them, for the wars seemed inevitable, and the rising hatred and tension in the city at once irrevocable and entirely avoidable. "This work," my friend said, "doesn't feed us, it breaks us. We don't know how to hope, and we recreate what has made us, over and over again. I think it's because we don't know how to love ourselves."

I wonder, now, if I'm even Appalachian, if this has been entirely supplanted by being a New Yorker. I wonder, am I actually trans, having so long lived as a man, or am I only, at this point, a man? I wonder how it is possible to psychically disinvest from the belief that I am white, when in this culture I will always be white. I wonder too, if the consideration of questions like these is at once utterly beside the point—and also *the* point.

There is a quote from the gnostic text "The Gospel of Thomas" that says that if you bring forth what is within you, it will save you, and that if you do not bring forth what is within you, it will destroy you.[3] Another way of understanding this quote, though, is that what destroys you can also save you. Oskar and I are still alive, and it is our destruction and dislocation that has also been our survival. Giving up parts of our inheritance has required us to understand them, and this simultaneous disinvestment and understanding have helped us claim, insofar as we've been able to claim it, our birthright. What destroyed me has also saved me—the place, the people, the culture that made me—and I am tired of the name I chose for myself, because it doesn't actually say what I am—it doesn't contain what I hope for.

I don't have a conclusion to this chapter—there is no final thought, because this is all in process, these formations and reformations of identity. I will say that I no longer live in the oscillations between beauty and terror, and I find that the middle ground of these, for me, is curiosity, and it seems this curiosity might be the foundational element for love.

NOTES

1   James Baldwin, "Introduction to Notes of a Native Son, 1984," in *Collected Essays*, edited by Toni Morrison (New York: Library of America, 1998), 808–13.

2   Jayne Ann Phillips, *Black Tickets* (New York: Vintage Books, 2001).

3   Marvin W. Meyer, ed., "The Gospel of Thomas with the Greek Gospel of Thomas," in *The Nag Hammadi Scriptures: The Revised and Updated Translation of Sacred Gnostic Texts* (New York: HarperOne, 2009), 133–56.

ABOUT THE AUTHOR

Tennessee Jones is a Brooklyn-based writer from Southern Appalachia. He is the author of the Lambda Award–nominated collection *Deliver Me from Nowhere*. His current novel-in-progress was named a finalist for the 2019 Creative Capital Award in Fiction and has received residency support from MacDowell, The Fine Arts Work Center, Lambda Literary Foundation, Lower Manhattan Cultural Council, and Phillips Exeter Academy. His fiction and essays have appeared in numerous publications including the *New York Times* and the *Believer*. He is currently studying trauma-informed somatic therapy at Silberman School of Social Work and divinity at Union Theological Seminary.

Queer Hills, Hollers, and Mountain People

Your Own Country: Finding Queer History in Johnson City, Tennessee

Samantha Allen

Queer history reminds me of the first drive I took through the Appalachian Mountains on a cloudy day in April 2013. When I looked in the rearview mirror, I could only see the terrain I traversed most recently: the last mountain pass I drove through, the nearest bend in the two-lane highway. Just beyond my vision lay countless rolling peaks, almost comforting in their seeming endlessness but ultimately out of reach. The LGBTQIA+ past is notoriously hard to access, passed down from generation to generation through oral history, journals, and memoirs. Exiled from many official sources, reduced to euphemism in others, we have had to tell our own stories in zines stretching from *Vice Versa* (1947–1948) through *Vector* (1964–1976) to *Original Plumbing* (2009–2019), scholarly journals like *GLQ* and the *Journal of Homosexuality*, and popular histories that are usually penned by members of the community.

We don't learn about Stonewall in schools; we have to piece together our knowledge of the riots from accounts like those found in the 2019 *The Stonewall Reader*. We don't encounter LGBTQIA+ history in textbooks; we have to seek out books like Michael Bronski's 2011 *A Queer History of the United States* or Cleve Jones's 2016 *When We Rise*. And, in part, because we have so much farther to go before we reach full queer liberation too few of us take the time to look backward. We keep our eyes on the road ahead.

On that spring day in 2013, I was on my way to Johnson City, Tennessee—a city of sixty thousand people that I knew nothing about, but that I would come to regard as a second home. I was living in Atlanta at the time and had made a friend over social media who invited me to take the five-hour drive north for a comic book convention held at East Tennessee State University. As I steered my faithful Honda Fit through the Smokies, its 4-cylinder engine struggling to summit even these forgiving slopes, I felt like I was on the brink of discovering some well-kept secret. Ahead of me was a town cool enough to bring the voice actor for Mario to its comic book convention but also a town that, in my solipsism, I assumed no one had heard of before, despite its prominent mention in the oft-covered song "Wagon Wheel." I had come out as a transgender woman in Atlanta the previous year and learned in short order that the city was teeming with fellow LGBTQIA+ people. (Even that fact was a surprise to me, as a relative newcomer to the American South.) But I still thought, foolishly and to my shame, that Tennessee was a homogeneously heterosexual wasteland. In the years to come, I was proven wonderfully wrong. But it was the years in Johnson City's rearview mirror that would surprise me most.

In 1985, nearly three decades before my first fateful drive north to Johnson City, a young man with AIDS was driving south from New York City to the same destination. His story serves as the opening anecdote for *My Own Country*, Dr. Abraham Verghese's popular 1994 memoir about treating HIV patients in Johnson City in the mid-1980s, at a time when many of his colleagues in Tennessee feared the virus and were resistant to treating openly gay men.[1] In vivid prose, Verghese imagines the young man's drive, picturing "how the road rises, sheer rock on one side," and how "the kudzu takes over, [seeming] to hold up a hillside."[2] The beauty of the geography stands in stark contrast to the man's mounting symptoms, his body overtaken with alternating fevers and chills. At last, he arrives in Johnson City, his hometown and also the place where he will die. "It would have all been familiar, this country," Verghese writes, "His own country."[3] The relief of his arrival is short-lived; before long, the young man finds himself in the emergency room of the Johnson City Medical Center, struggling to breathe. His lungs give out, and doctors flood the hallway as they rush to his side. Thanks to their efforts, he wakes up, only to find a tube in his throat. "He must have wondered if this was hell," Verghese writes.[4] The young man is brought back from the brink of death—but a mere three weeks later, he is irrevocably gone.

My heart ached when I read this story for the first time, not just because of its tragic end—and not just because it showcases the pain and confusion of the AIDS crisis in its early days—but because I ran across it a full seven years after Johnson City had already become my idea of queer heaven. I had been so unaware of the history behind this place I loved. At that comic book convention in 2013, I met Jennifer Culp, a bisexual artist and writer, who became my closest friend. The small house she shared with her husband, Justin Mitchell, wasn't exactly on my way from Atlanta to New York City—a drive I did with regularity—but I was so eager to befriend Jenn and so enamored with Johnson City that I made it my go-to stop. In short visits spread months apart, I experienced Johnson City's queerness in snippets. On one visit, Jenn and Justin took me to the New Beginnings nightclub, a gay bar that sits unassumingly between auto dealers on the outskirts of the city, its thrumming interior a world apart from the building's industrial surroundings. On another visit, they introduced me to a cadre of queer artists and crafters that seemed to grow each time I left town and came back. We would all go out downtown, drink, and take selfies in the grungy, overdecorated bathroom at the Hideaway nightclub. (Once at the Hideaway, with my hair in pigtails and my face made out to look like Harley Quinn, I took runner-up in the costume contest at an event known as "Goth Prom." It remains my proudest achievement.)

I couldn't get enough of Johnson City, this weird mélange of conservative and liberal America, a college town in the heart of the Bible Belt, not quite as hip as Asheville, North Carolina, but also free from that larger city's hype. When I wrote my own memoir, *Real Queer America: LGBT Stories from Red States*, in 2017, I devoted a whole chapter to Johnson City, but to the Johnson City of today.[5] Mine was a very presentist memoir, short on history and focused, perhaps to a fault, on the progressive impact that queer people will continue to have on more conservative parts of the United States. I was so intent on letting my readers know how LGBTQIA+-friendly Johnson City could feel *now, today*—so adamant on correcting the misperceptions I once held about queer life in states like Georgia and Tennessee, and that I knew many coastal readers still held—that I never stopped to think about how Johnson City got that way. It wasn't until after my book was published that my friend Jeff Clark, a local lefty politico who ran for city commission, told me about *My Own Country*.

"Do you know the history behind why a little Appalachian city like this has such a strong gay community?" Jeff asked me.

"I always assumed it was the influence of being a college town," I said. "Is there something more to it?"

He showed me the *New York Times* book review of *My Own Country*, informing me that, thanks to Dr. Abraham Verghese's willingness to treat HIV/AIDS patients in the 1980s, Johnson City Medical Center had been one of the only places in the region where openly gay men felt comfortable seeking treatment.[6] (Indeed, in *My Own Country*, Dr. Verghese—who is straight—often specifies how many miles his patients would travel specifically to see him, speculating that they may have felt more comfortable under his care because he too was a cultural outsider, a man with Indian parents born in Ethiopia now living in East Tennessee.) I was shocked I hadn't heard his story before. I felt like Jeff had handed me the key to a puzzle box. Dr. Verghese didn't fully explain the current strength of Johnson City's LGBTQIA+ community—like any small city, it has many queer pioneers, both sung and unsung—but it undoubtedly made a difference that I was still able to feel on a gut level three decades later. There was something different about this place. Something special in its already unique mix.

"I feel like this history isn't brought up enough," Jeff told me nonchalantly, while I was still trying to absorb the new information, unaware that he had just blown my mind. "So the more people that know the better."

After that conversation with Jeff, I bought—and inhaled—*My Own Country*, my eyes lighting up with recognition every time I spotted familiar landmarks in the pages of that text. In the 1980s, Johnson City's downtown was deteriorating, and Dr. Verghese regularly references its state of disrepair. Because rent was more affordable downtown then, that is where the local Tri-City AIDS Project support group first sought out office space, as Dr. Verghese recounts.[7] By the time I started visiting Johnson City in 2013, the downtown was in the midst of its recent revitalization, full of bustling bars, restaurants, and breweries that were taking out leases on Main Street's 1920s-era buildings with their gorgeous, Chicagoesque façades. It never occurred to me that the bar where I came *this* close to winning the Goth Prom costume contest might have been just down the street from the place where Johnson City AIDS patients once went looking for solace. Sadly, as Dr. Verghese notes, the Tri-City AIDS Project support group was denied their desired downtown office space after the owner learned that people with AIDS would be entering his property. They settled for a space a few blocks away on Spring Street instead.[8]

Near the start of *My Own Country*, Dr. Verghese ventures into a local gay bar called the Connection—the predecessor of New Beginnings—to deliver a presentation on AIDS to a group of curious but also quietly scared patrons. He remembers how some Johnson City residents who lived near the Connection would sometimes "express their disapproval" with the gay bar by committing acts of vandalism in the parking lot, "with brickbats thrown at a windshield or by slashing tires."[9] I felt retroactive embarrassment at having just blithely strolled into New Beginnings with my friends all those years later and ordering a drink without stopping to consider that the bar might have as long or as interesting of a queer history as any longstanding nightlife hotspot in San Francisco's Castro District. I regretted not respecting—or even investigating—the past that I had sensed beneath Johnson City's surface, playing underneath the music.

When I finally put the book down, I asked Jenn if Dr. Verghese was a household name in Johnson City, feeling not so much betrayed that she had never told me about him as disappointed in myself that I had never directly asked her about Johnson City's LGBTQIA+ history. High on the newness of my discovery, I was adamant that Dr. Verghese should be recognized somehow. There should be a statue of him in Founders Park downtown! A street named after him! Or, at least, a cocktail called "The Abraham" at New Beginnings! Jenn told me that older people in Johnson City's medical world still know his name, as do LGBTQIA+ leaders in town, but "not so much the super young'ns."

"We do not learn about him in school or anything, that's for sure," she joked.

Jenn was right: as queer people, we are so used to being omitted from history that the very idea of hearing about someone like Dr. Verghese in a public school is a laughable one. As of this writing, only five states—California, New Jersey, Colorado, Oregon, and Illinois—require school curricula to be LGBTQIA+-inclusive.[10] In fact, an even larger number of states—six of them—expressly restrict the discussion of LGBTQIA+ topics in schools through "Don't Say Gay" or "No Promo Homo" laws, as the Movement Advancement Project notes.[11] (Tennessee is not one of the six, but two of its neighbors to the south, Mississippi and Alabama, are.) Decreasing the likelihood of Dr. Verghese being mentioned during K–12 education is the fact that Tennessee is an abstinence-only sex education state by law; teachers might be understandably fearful of mentioning someone whose name is so intimately associated with rural AIDS. A few years ago, social media had a heyday with the fact that a *RuPaul's Drag Race* star thought people had died during the Stonewall riots, but that's exactly the kind of thing that happens when LGBTQIA+ people are left out of textbooks and lesson plans. Everyone learns straight history; few learn queer history unless they expressly seek it out.

It's a testament to our queer resilience that, even though we are often disconnected from our past, we still manage to transform our surroundings through sheer force of will and strategic organizing. In September 2018, Johnson City held its first Pride parade, and a staggering ten thousand people attended, walking and dancing through the town's main drags.[12] The same downtown where the Tri-City AIDS Project support group was once turned away now opened its doors wide to queer folks. I wish that first generation of AIDS patients in Johnson City could have lived to see the photos of that inaugural Pride. The very street that rejected them, now filled with rainbows and Pride flags and same-sex couples holding hands. When I asked Jason Willis, a member of the executive council for the LGBTQIA+ organization TriPride—which also serves nearby Kingsport and Bristol—how that seemingly miraculous event had come into existence, he had a straightforward answer. Surely it had been the result of years of planning and foresight, I thought. Not so.

"TriPride was formed unofficially by a group of like-minded friends in October 2017," he told me. "And basically we came together to see if there was any support to do a full-fledged proper Pride for the Tri-Cities region." Less than a year later, East Tennessee State University's football stadium wouldn't have been able to hold all the people who showed up to that inaugural Pride celebration. How many of those people, I wondered, knew about Johnson City's unique history during the HIV/AIDS crisis?

"Honestly, I don't know if a whole lot of people do," Willis told me, but that's not necessarily for lack of trying. During that first Pride Week, as the *Johnson City Press* reported, sections from the AIDS Memorial Quilt were displayed at a local museum.[13] Willis told me that they had specifically sought out some of the panels "that were from this area that had not been here since they were made and sent off." In a beautiful bit of archival luck, *My Own Country* actually captures the moment those quilt panels were seemingly made: a night when members of the Tri-City AIDS Project gathered inside a member's trailer out on McCray Road and held a sewing party, following the specifications handed down from the NAMES Project, the national organization that oversaw the creation of the Quilt.

"I tell you, I don't want my name on no quilt," one member reportedly said.

"Well, you have to be dead first, so don't worry about it," came the gallows humor retort.[14]

Those quilt panels traveled through time and all around the country only to return, however briefly, to the city where they were made on the eve of its Pride Parade, literally stitching the past and future of Johnson City's queer community together into a single fabric. Anyone in attendance at that museum event heard about "Dr. V," as he is affectionately called by those in the know.

"He was brought up some then," Willis remembered. "Other than that, it's just word of mouth and sharing this history."

If there's anyone in Johnson City who's spreading that word, it's Jon Tully, a local teacher who first caught wind of Dr. V from older gay friends in the area. (Jenn introduced me to Jon over schnitzel at the German restaurant Freiberg's during my most recent weekend in Johnson City.) "I've told more people than I've heard it from," Jon told me. "I've told a couple hundred people, but I've only heard it from maybe two or three individuals."

For Jon and his husband Zach Armistead, who works locally in the health care industry, learning about *My Own Country* was the same kind of epiphany it had been for me: "Before we heard that fact, we just assumed, 'Oh, Johnson City's a college town, and so it's bound to be more on the liberal side of [LGBTQIA+ issues],' but that second piece—that historical piece—is when it just clicked into place." Now, all of us see Johnson City through new eyes: as a city where queer folks once fought against a virus and died, but died with a little more dignity thanks to Dr. V, and as a city where the queer folks of today are using their lives to advocate for liberation. It is both places at once, their topographies overlaid on top of each other.

Today, when I think about the harrowing drive that the young man from the start of *My Own Country* took in 1985, I also think about a much more hopeful drive that my new friend Jon Tully took to Johnson City in 2008.

In the fall of 2005, when they were both attending colleges in Tennessee three hours apart, Jon and Zach met for the first time at a murder mystery–themed costume party in Maryville. Zach wasn't out of the closet yet, and Jon was still in ex-gay therapy. Jon was gregarious and Zach was the definition of a wallflower, but the unlikely pair was forced to spend much of that night together, because Jon had been assigned to come as Cleopatra, and Zach was told to come as, of course, Mark Antony. The game called for these two historical lovers to interact with each other, exchange clues, and help solve the crime. That didn't happen. Jon's Cleopatra drag costume, which involved a bedsheet and balloons, was so bad that "it was bordering on political activism," as he told me. Zach, for his part, wasn't quite sure what to do with "this very outrageous person" standing in front of him, so he retreated into his shell, as Jon grew frustrated with his unresponsiveness. Suffice it to say, the night didn't end in the same passionate way that the real-life Cleopatra and Mark Anthony would have ended theirs. Zach went back to Johnson City, Jon to Cleveland, Tennessee.

Still, Jon persistently pursued a friendship with the much shyer guy, talking with him on Facebook intermittently for the next two years, their long-distance conversations growing more intimate. In the meantime, Zach came out. Jon left ex-gay therapy, having come "very close to a psychic break" but ultimately making it "through the wilderness," as he described it to me. The star-crossed lovers arranged to see each other in person again at a Borders books in Knoxville during their senior year. This wasn't their forever just yet; they were only trying to see if the connection they had forged online would feel as strong in person.

Jon relayed the story of their reunion to me almost cinematically: "The automatic doors opened, and the sun was setting through the glass, so it was only [Zach's] silhouette, honey, walking through that door in slow motion, and I saw him, and I thought, 'Phew, I don't have feelings, this is great'... Then, of course, I got home that night and it just walloped me over the head."

They started a relationship but were still long-distance until graduation. The very day Jon threw his cap in the air in the summer of 2008, his car was already packed. Jon must have been giddy, willing to break the speed limit a bit to get to his boyfriend that much sooner. He drove three hours through the Tennessee hills from Cleveland to Johnson City to start his life with Zach—but that life, I realize more deeply now, was made possible in part by the queer people who bravely died here and the doctor who cared for them as they did.

Every so often on the narrow highways that take you to Johnson City, a sign prompts you to turn off at an overlook. Doing so adds some time to your drive. Sometimes, like Jon, you're in a hurry to get to where you're going, but if you stop, get out of your car, breathe the crisp air, and walk to the edge of the railing—or often, a knee-high stone wall—you can see the Appalachian Mountains stretching forever behind you, covered in sugar maple and beech trees. From high enough, the peaks don't obscure each other. You can't trace the road behind you perfectly, but you can see more or less where you came from, and a preview of where you're going. Learning LGBTQIA+ history similarly takes a bit of time; it's not something that we can absorb through osmosis in the school system or trust our country to honor. But it can render a place like Johnson City—like any place you love—dense with meaning, rich with pastness, and rife with potential for the future. It is how you make a place your own country.

NOTES

1   Abraham Verghese, *My Own Country: A Doctor's Story* (New York: Vintage, 1995).
2   Ibid., 5–6.
3   Ibid., 6.
4   Ibid., 9.
5   Samantha Allen, *Real Queer America: LGBT Stories from Red States* (New York: Little, Brown, 2019).
6   Perri Klass, "AIDS in the Heartland," *New York Times*, August 28, 1994, accessed October 6, 2021, https://www.nytimes.com/1994/08/28/books/aids-in-the-heartland.html.
7   Verghese, *My Own Country*, 351–52.
8   Ibid., 352.
9   Ibid., 53.
10   Harron Walker, "Here's Every State That Requires Schools to Teach LGBTQ+ History," *Out*, August 16, 2019, accessed October 6, 2021, https://www.out.com/news/2019/8/16/heres-every-state-requires-schools-teach-lgbtq-history.
11   "Safe Schools Laws," Movement Advancement Project, accessed October 6, 2021, https://www.lgbtmap.org/equality-maps/safe_school_laws.
12   Ashley Sharp, "10,000 Celebrate Inaugural Tri-Pride Festival in Johnson City," WJHL, September 15, 2018, accessed October 6, 2021, https://www.wjhl.com/news/local/10000-celebrate-inaugural-tri-pride-festival-in-johnson-city.
13   Jessica Fuller, "You Don't Have to Wait Until Saturday to Celebrate: TriPride Brings Week of Events," *Johnson City Press*, September 10, 2018, accessed October 6, 2021, https://tinyurl.com/cjcaz8jc.
14   Verghese, *My Own Country*, 406.

ABOUT THE AUTHOR

Samantha Allen is the author of *Real Queer America: LGBT Stories from Red States* and *Love & Estrogen*. She is a GLAAD Award-winning journalist whose work has been published by the *New York Times*, CNN, and more. She holds a PhD in Women's, Gender, and Sexuality Studies from Emory University.

Home Grown: Critical Queer Activism in Appalachia and the South

Heather Brydie Harris

> I am a sleeping giant.
> There lives a riot in my bones.
> I am a mouth full of seed.
> I am a quiet indigo dawn.
> —Suzi Q. Smith, "Sleeping Giant"

Queer. I discovered queer when I was seventeen years old and attending college, nestled in the Smoky Mountains outside Asheville. There, although I had known gay for years, I found queer. Queer came to me in the form of femme solidarity, stone-cold butch protections, learning to drink moonshine out of a jug, and the activism of my professor who sent more books to the nearest prison than she assigned for her classes. Queer came to me also in form. The form and gentle slope of well-fed Southern women in cotton t-shirts and jeans rolled at the cuff who had histories of convictions for trespassing, protesting, and resisting both state-sanctioned and interpersonal violence in all its many forms. Queer came to me in sound. In the violent crash of naked bodies in cool natural pools, the soft hum of feet padding the ground on the way to eat scrambled tofu, farm-grown greens, and slow-cooked meats. The chant, hum, clap, sway, and thundering stomp of protest songs. Queer was sensual, sacred, shifting, and social. Unlike other identities I had come to know up until that point, the ones that gave me momentary comfort and were handed down to me like so many secondhand labels, queer was self-imposed. It originated from the body, but a larger body of people made it at once possible, tangible, and legible.

Queer was demanding. It demanded a critical gaze be cast on any violent social system that seemed unbreakable, and it demanded it be broken. It demanded action by those very bodies who had been crushed the most, not only by queerphobia, homophobia, transphobia, and cissexism, but also by racism, classism, sexism, and xenophobia. It demanded that those crushed voices and bodies lead the change. Queer didn't call for silent comfort but for a stirring up, a flipping over and examining of all the parts of every societal machination, including constructs and systems of oppression.

In my life, queer still demands. I have come to understand queer's cry (often emerging unexpectedly from my own throat) as an insistence upon critical interventions within discourses and social systems that insist upon injustice. I find the demand growing ever stronger as a Black nonbinary activist-scholar learning and living in the South. As I sit, writing and revising these paragraphs, reports of two more mass shootings fill my newsfeed.[1] Babies, children, youth, adults, and families sit, sleep, and wait in cages.[2] Millions of Americans have undrinkable water.[3] More Black transgender women, our sisters, have been murdered.[4] And these are only some of the current devastating crises occurring in a small area of the globe that are rooted in white supremacy, heterosexism, transphobia, and violent state-powered forms of colonization-era patriarchy.

With a frightening rise in hate crimes across the United States within the past three years, social justice organizations within rural, Appalachian, and Southern locations have had increasing work to do to combat individual, as well as institutional and structural, forms of violence. This chapter, using queer and Black feminist methodologies, pays particular attention to the intersectional and multi-issue organizing done by queer organizers across ethnicity, race, and gender expression and identity. This chapter also works to queer notions of space and place by naming Appalachia and the South as cradles of social change, subverting the common idea that radical queer activism occurs primarily in urban areas.

In beginning this chapter with my own experiences of queerness and Appalachia, I intend to draw the reader to two points that may not be readily clear. First, that queer histories do not begin and end in major coastal metropolitan areas, and, second, that what we consider to be credible academic sources should and must include the very people that occupy and experience these overlooked spaces. Within the first point, I am pointing to Appalachia, the South, and rural areas as their own sites of queer historicity. These places are not, as some might suspect, merely beneficiaries of urban efforts to garner state-sanctioned legal rights and greater freedoms. The discourse that queer liberation efforts begin and end outside of Appalachian, Southern, and rural areas is dangerous as it continues the narrative that Appalachia/the South/rural areas are backward, more conservative, undereducated, and/or helpless victims needing to be saved. Part of the discourse about these particular places and groups of people is how they are being recorded, or left out of, the historical archive. Negative, false, or skewed discourse about these regions is especially dangerous considering the large population of people of color in these areas, who, through racialization, already contend with damning discourses that impact their daily lives.

Scholar activism has a responsibility to function as a critical intervention, disrupting marginalizing discourses that work to depict these regions as victim and/or passive beneficiary. Writing, and rewriting, queer histories that center the activist histories of these regions counteracts the harmful and undelineating work of outsider-dominant depictions of the people, efforts, and successes of these areas. Within my second point, I place myself at the center of my own understanding of what it means to be queer and to perform the act of queering, which I came to understand as a form of activism and a way to disrupt unjust systems of power. This second point deals with issues of legitimacy and authority. Writing ourselves, that is the very people-dominant discourses and written histories often objectify, marginalize, wrongly interpret, or even falsely portray, back into the archive is itself a scholar-activist project. Scholar-activism that rewrites activist histories, such as E. Patrick Johnson's *Black. Queer. Southern. Women: An Oral History* (2018), serves, then, as a corrective to the assumption that liberation efforts occur in East and West Coast cities, while the South remains regressive.

In fact, radical queer activism, often linked to social movements taking place in the 1960s and 1970s in metropolitan cities on the Northeast and West Coasts, has a long and compelling history outside of these areas. While there remains connective tissues that form abstract relations between queer movement work in places like New York City and San Francisco, on the one hand, and the South and Appalachia, on the other, the latter regions have developed distinct organizational forms, tactics, and practices that are derived from their unique social and historical contexts.

Exploitation of natural resources, including the exploitation of the earth and of human labor, and the diverse ethnoscapes that have taken shape both from human migration and the human trafficking and enslavement of Africans and subsequent resistance traditions have informed activist strategies in these regions. Here, the term "ethnoscapes" refers to the movement of various groups of people who, through migration, form new political, racial, and cultural landscapes in the places they move to and through.[5] The resistance to and backlash to these above conditions, namely enslavement, exploitation, and migration, have created a social justice culture that is at once vibrant, radical, and robust, as well as sidelined from the hegemonic, or dominant, memory and present awareness. This sidelining is due, in part, to historians favoring of neoliberal "successes" (specifically single-issue and reactionary laws, such as same-gender marriage, or the passing of hate crime legislation) over multi-issue, grassroots, radical, interracial, and queer-led social justice–based coalitions that are concerned with root causes.[6] The latter has come to be the basis of many Appalachian and Southern organizations. Moreover, with a frightening rise in hate crimes across the United States over the past three years, social justice organizations within rural, Appalachian, and Southern locations have had increasing work to do to combat individual, as well as institutional and structural, forms of violence that take place in these areas.[7]

Recently, I had the pleasure of interviewing two long-time social justice organizers in Louisville, Kentucky, who have both played active roles at the Highlander Research and Education Center and beyond. Carol Kraemer is a former organizational manager at the Fairness Campaign and Yer Girlfriend band member, who has also been active in Showing Up for Racial Justice (SURJ) Louisville. Highlander Research and Education Center, formerly Highlander Folk School, was founded in 1932 and has been a bastion of social justice training and cultural organizing since, with an active role during the civil rights movement. The Fairness Campaign was founded in Louisville, Kentucky, in 1991, as an LGBTQIA+ equality and advocacy organization working primarily to pass LGBTQIA+ antidiscrimination ordinances across Kentucky. Pam McMichael is now retired from working as the executive director at Highlander for twelve years and is a founding codirector of Southerners on New Ground (SONG), which was founded in 1993. Both have helped shape the climate of radical queer activism in the Southern and Appalachian regions of the US. Pam McMichael describes SONG, Highlander, and other social justice organizations in the South as being based on a we're-all-in-this-together mindset that attempts to move equality and social justice efforts forward without leaving anyone behind.[8] This centeredness on we're-all-in-this-together, coalition-based activism translates into practice by first acknowledging that all oppressive systems are connected, while emphasizing individual stories and analyses as critical to the organizing work.[9] Similarly, Carol Kraemer conceptualizes queer justice work as part and parcel of economic and racial justice organizing.

This emphasis on organizing along lines of difference as a collective has caused organizations in the South and Appalachia to experience violent backlash. On March 29, 2019, the Highlander Research and Education Center in New Market, Tennessee, was the target of an attack due to their long history of social justice activism that centers participatory action research, popular education, and mutual aid among communities from Appalachia and the South.[10] In the early morning, a fire burned down the main administrative building at the Highlander Center.[11] During the investigation a white power symbol was found spray-painted in the parking lot. No lives were lost and nobody was injured in the fire; however, many were shaken, including the hundreds of people who have been touched directly by Highlander's presence and perseverance throughout its nearly ninety years of existence. This was not the first attack on Highlander. Throughout the organization's lifespan, Highlander has been the target of violent actions and threats that have ranged from red-baiting to individual and state-sanctioned acts of violence committed against both property and people, including removal of licensure and land.

Hate crime reporting has increased steadily over the past three years in the US and continues to rise.[12] The arson attack at Highlander took place in the same month as Black churches were burned, families were ripped apart in detention centers, and videos were going viral on social media of police brutalizing Black and other children of color at school. Although there is nothing redemptive in the loss of life, destruction of records, or suffering of Black, Brown, queer, poor, or disabled bodies in the South and Appalachia, the social justice traditions that have risen up are transformed by it, as are the places and spaces in which it is being done. Formations of Southern Blackness gave rise to E. Patrick Johnson's conception of "quare": a queer Black person with Southern sensibilities in Black vernacular. Likewise, racial and gendered dimensions, economic realities, and cultural forms gave rise to queer, or quare, organizing that is distinctly Southern, Appalachian, queer, race-centered, and multi-issue in a way that speaks true for, and echoes, the lives of the people of these regions.[13] Within Johnson's multipoint definition of quare he writes, "One who thinks and feels and acts (and, sometimes, 'acts up'); committed to struggle against all forms of oppression—racial, gender, class, religious, etc."[14] This definition of quare captures a theory in the flesh, a theory that is embodied and practiced based on the dimensions of our own physical and environmental circumstances.[15]

Pam McMichael, prompted to do a word association when thinking of Highlander, offered these words: "Simple and complicated. Beautiful. Powerful. Hard. Expectation. History. Future. Love. Smoky Mountains on your horizon. Did I say sunrises and sunsets? Foggy mornings. A place people call home who haven't even been there. A place people connect for decades. An important place because of people. It's always about people."[16] Pam described Highlander as being like an infinity symbol, those who come to Highlander take something back to their communities, and others from that community return and give back to Highlander, and the cycle continues.[17] This site of popular education, where people come to learn from one another, share the situations impacting their communities, and work toward collective social change, has become a bastion of both hope and home for many in the region.

Carol Kraemer, reflecting on why people have wanted to take Highlander down over the decades said, "It was a dangerous thing to have a place where black and white folks could come together and build a movement. That was dangerous."[18] Highlander has become a place where civil rights icons, labor organizers from Appalachia, masculine of center queer women, and radical faeries can gather, become community, and work collectively toward shared ends. These efforts, often in the form of cultural organizing, coupled with art, performance, music, and song, become attuned to what José Muñoz called "disidentification."[19] Disidentification is a way that people, particularly queer people of color, negotiate the dominant culture through enacting performance and performative expressions that are architectonic and world-making. In other words, disidentification is not simply an individual act but a resistance strategy that is capable of building alternative and counterspaces. Disidentification is not against or for majority cultural values, rather, it queers the norms associated with hegemonic values and uses them within performance, to create new worlds.

While Highlander is not a queer organization per se (nor is it not), those who make Highlander the space it is are participating in what Dean Spade calls "critical queer and trans politics."[20] This politic is in opposition to single-issue gay and lesbian politics that are focused on inclusion and rights; rather, it is a critical queer and trans politic that looks for solutions to systemic problems that have their roots buried deep in racism, classism, sexism, homophobia, and ableism. While inclusion and rights are often the basis of organizations associated with large metropolitan networks and task forces, many of these organizations are prone to using the same mechanisms of change as the systems utilized to enact violence, such as a heavy reliance on legislative change within the current system vs. a title restructuring of the system itself. As Audre Lorde said, "What does it mean when the tools of a racist patriarchy are used to examine the fruits of that same patriarchy? It means that only the most narrow perimeters of change are possible and allowable."[21]

Much of the queer organizing that is done throughout Appalachia and the South (Highlander is but one example), is aligned with a critical queer and trans politic stemming from theories in the flesh and realities of both place and space. Organizations and coalitions have created ideological frameworks that are not tied to specific structures and human constructions, like buildings that may burn. These social change frameworks are carried through the embodied praxis of the people. It is this performed embodiment of a critical queer homegrown activism that is architectonic, or world-building. Highlander flourishes exactly because of the queer expressions, epistemologies, and performances it engenders—queer voices singing together, radical faeries in full-face singing "Aint You Got a Right" and butch hands teaching and building chairs out of pallets.[22] Queer activism understands our bodies as sites of resistance. It acknowledges the way the physical forms but also the fictions (and discourses) of our beings' code and contour space. It acknowledges that the way we take up space, as well as where and how we take it up, becomes either in submission to, opposition to, or disidentification with the constriction of state normalizing logics on our identities and lives.

Critical queer Southern and Appalachian activism that comes from the people who live t/here represents a refusal to concede to normalizing logics and dominant ideologies that mal-distribute resources (including the resources of whiteness, cisness, and heterosexuality, and even urbanity). Queer organizing that works to move beyond recognition, inclusion, and rights and toward collective transformation predicated on a collective privileging of intersectional activism that seeks to root out systemic injustice is world-making.

The many crises currently inundating our personal, political, and social lives make it clear why we can't passively wait for this new world to begin. The call of queer justice work grows ever more demanding. It begins with our individual lives, understanding how our own identities, environments, and experiences work to form a theory in the flesh. It extends to a larger body formed of those who will make our queerness both legible and applicable—those who will join us in demanding not only the change of violent systems but an interrogation of the root causes of social violence. This demand extends increasingly to our scholarship, and at the same time scholarship within academia must be queered/quared. It cannot remain comfortable, clinging to a politic of inclusion but, rather, must be committed to deconstructing current systems, practices, and knowledge traditions that are not focused on 1) critically interrogating everything that is hegemonic for deeply embedded violent roots and 2) rebuilding and creating new epistemologies based on intersectional, multi-issue work that is expressed through a queer/trans politic. It won't be easy. To queer (verb) is a dangerous thing. Yet scholar-activism housed within a queer ethic and social justice politic when done fearlessly (as Cherríe Moraga once told me scholar-activism must be done) can aid in undoing the damage that state-sanctioned violence, state-controlled memorializing, and neoliberal successes have put in place.

This chapter began with my own reflection on coming to understand my queer identity and my call to queer (analyze and disrupt) unjust systems. Starting with the self, specifically my queer Black self that is writing here in Appalachia, is a practice of reflexivity, as well as a radical praxis that insists upon the nonhegemonic self as a worthwhile subject for intellectual consideration. Writing from my own center is only the beginning; part and parcel of activist scholarship is correcting the collective memory that is held around movements. Positioning the South and Appalachia as critical to social justice movement history and present practice creates a counter to the dominant discourse regarding where and how change occurs. Re/understanding the historical and political geographies of these places and the people—the lives, experiences, and physical bodies of those that live t/here—as already having their own distinct and uniquely informed activist histories is part of the responsibility of activist scholarship. This chapter posits these places and groups as not merely victims of oppressive systemic measures or simply beneficiaries of urban, single-issue, and often state-sanctioned rights. Instead, I argue that because of the distinct racial, political, historical, economic, etc. landscape of the lives of those who have lived, or are living, in these areas, a historicity emerges that is set apart from many single-issue efforts associated with largely Northeastern and metropolitan areas. The Highlander Center has been used as but one example of an Appalachian-located and people-powered organization with a long history of multi-issue, coalition and community–led social change work. While efforts have been made to begin unearthing and highlighting activist histories in these regions, there is still much work to be done. Activist-scholars have a responsibility to correct marginalizing dominant discourse that functions to skew, mute, erase, or render certain histories as illegible. Queering the archive is a demanding academic task, but one we must continuously undertake if we are truly invested in disrupting all forms of oppression. The act of writing, rewriting, correcting, and intervening in harmful dominating discourses is the practice of activist scholarship.

NOTES

1   Meg Wager, Elise Hammond, Mike Hayes, and Veronica Rocha, "At Least 31 Killed in US Weekend Mass Shootings," CNN, August 5, 2019, accessed October 6, 2021, https://www.cnn.com/us/live-news/el-paso-dayton-shootings-august-2019/index.html.

2   "Separation of Families at the Border—Overview and Update," National Network for Immigrant and Refugee Rights, accessed October 6, 2021, https://tinyurl.com/nayxp9x8.

3   George Goehl, "Can the US's Unsafe Water Crisis Unite Americans?" *Guardian*, April 8, 2019, accessed October 6, 2021, https://www.theguardian.com/commentisfree/2019/apr/08/us-unsafe-water-crisis-unite-americans.

4   "Violence against the Transgender Community in 2019," Human Rights Campaign, accessed October 6, 2021, https://www.hrc.org/resources/violence-against-the-transgender-community-in-2019.

5   Arjun Appadurai, "Disjuncture and Difference in the Global Cultural Economy," *Theory, Culture & Society* 7, nos. 2–3 (June 1990): 295–310.

6   For an example of how a focus on neoliberal success distorts historical memory, see Jackson Wright Shultz and Kristopher Shultz, "Queer and Trans After Obergefell v. Hodges: An Autoethnographic Oral History," *Humboldt Journal of Social Relations* 38 (2016): 46–61.

7   Devlin Barrett, "Hate Crimes Rose 17 Percent Last Year, According to New FBI Data," *Washington Post*, November 13, 2018, accessed October 6, 2021, https://tinyurl.com/b8jzhztk.

8   Pam McMichael, "Highlander Interview," interviewed by Heather Brydie Harris, University of Louisville, March 4, 201.

9   Ibid.

10   Sarah Jones, "At Famed Civil-Rights Center, Fire Destroys a Building, but Not a Mission," *Intelligencer*, April 6, 2019, accessed October 6, 2021, https://nymag.com/intelligencer/2019/04/highlander-center-fire-destroys-building-not-its-mission.html.

11   Ibid.

12   John Eligon, "Hate Crimes Increase for the Third Consecutive Year, F.B.I. Reports," *New York Times*, November 13, 2018, accessed October 6, 2021, https://www.nytimes.com/2018/11/13/us/hate-crimes-fbi-2017.html.

13   E. Patrick Johnson, "'Quare' Studies, or (Almost) Everything I Know I Learned from My Grandmother," in *Black Queer Studies: A Critical Anthology*, edited by E. Patrick Johnson and Mae G. Henderson (Durham, NC: Duke University Press, 2005), 125.

14   Ibid.

15   Cherríe Moraga, "Theory in the Flesh," in *This Bridge Called Our Backs: Writings by Radical Women of Color*, 4th ed., edited by Cherríe Moraga and Gloria Anzaldúa (New York: State University of New York Press, 2015).

16   Pam McMichael, "Highlander Interview."

17   Ibid.

18   Carol Kraemer, "Southern Activism Interview," interviewed by Heather Brydie Harris, University of Louisville, February 18, 2019.

19   José Muñoz, *Disidentification: Queers of Color and the Performance of Politics* (Minneapolis: University of Minnesota Press, 1994).

20   Dean Spade, *Normal Life: Administrative Violence, Critical Trans Politics, and the Limits of Law* (Durham, NC: Duke University Press, 2015).

21   Audre Lorde, *Undersong: Chosen Poems Old and New* (London: Virago, 1993).

22   Carol Kraemer, "Southern Activism Interview."

ABOUT THE AUTHOR

Heather Brydie Harris is a PhD candidate in Pan-African Studies at the University of Louisville. They hold an MA in Social Justice and Ethics from Iliff School of Theology and Women and a BA in Gender Studies from Metropolitan State University of Denver. Brydie is a Black, multiracial, nonbinary femme poet, and scholar-activist. Their interests and research are based in the queer Black experience through the framework of womanist and quare theology via transcontinental social justice imaginaries and Afrofuturistic thought.

Rainbow Aging: Negotiating Queer Identities among Aging Central Appalachians

M. Aaron Guest

> We just have to be careful. Ya know? I never wanted to be in the closet, but people come to me now and ask what they should do, and I tell them don't. They don't need to deal with all of that here. There is too much. I wouldn't wish it on anyone . . . the young people today have it just as bad. They have basically forgotten about me, because I am old, but when they come and ask what they should do, I tell them don't come out. It was so bad for me. I haven't forgotten that. I mean they sent me through hell. I was one of the first ones out up here. I came out, because I knew what I wanted to be. . . I just realized what I was and didn't want to live a lie. But if people ask me, I tell them don't. It was hard. I think it has gotten worse for the young people with that guy in the office. Everyone started being full of hate again.
>
> —Frank, age fifty-seven, living in Appalachian Kentucky[1]

As the population of the United States continues to age, reaching over 20 percent of the population over age sixty-five by 2030, the diversity of the aging population will increase.[2] There are more lesbian, gay, bisexual, transgender, and queer (LGBTQIA+) individuals entering older age than ever before.[3] An estimated 2.4 million of the 39 million people in the US over age sixty-five are thought to self-identify as LGBTQIA+—a number expected to double by 2030.[4] Even though roughly 25 percent of the aging population live in rural environments, little attention has been given to their experiences.[5] Even less has examined the experiences of aging LGBTQIA+ Appalachians.

Appalachian scholarship on queer identities has focused on the experience of youth and emerging adults, particularly within the socioeconomic context of the changing region.[6] The emphasis on youth has somewhat negated the experience of those who have aged in the region as lesbian, gay, bisexual, transgender, questioning, or queer and in many ways removed their experiences from the cultural dialogue. Aging LGBTQIA+ individuals in Appalachia have navigated complex intersecting identities across their lifespan, as they seek to negotiate what it means to be "LGBTQIA+" and "Appalachian" in a cultural context that dichotomizes these identities.

This chapter aims to address that gap and to introduce the aging experiences of LGBTQIA+ Appalachians. The experiences, challenges, and opportunities identified come from four years of fieldwork and data collection in Appalachian Kentucky and West Virginia.[7] Countless individuals shared their experiences, their stories, their dreams, and their fears. I am grateful for their participation and their willingness to share in the hope it will create a more just world.

LGBTQIA+ Aging in Appalachia

Appalachia is often viewed as a homogenous region of shared identity. Discourses of Appalachia present a monolithic view of a religious, political, and cultural region. The image of a mountain cabin-dwelling people engrained by President Lyndon B. Johnson's War on Poverty has been supplemented by images of angry coal dust–covered miners demanding a second industrial revolution powered by fossil fuels.[8] Scarce attention has been given by those outside of the region to the infinite diversity that exists within the region.[9] Instead, a one-size-fits-all image of Appalachia is presented that silences the voices of marginalized populations. Embedded within these popular discourses are assumptions regarding sexuality, race, and religion. A single view of a white, heteronormative, Protestant region emerged. As this volume demonstrates, the reality of Appalachia is starkly different. Appalachia is a melting pot. It is a region connected by a shared culture, similar experiences of economic extraction, and, of course, constructed political boundaries.[10] Beyond the rhetoric presented in national media, Appalachia consists of people of all political affiliations, sexualities, religions, and races/ethnicities.

Central Appalachia is most often evoked when discussing the region—it is Central Appalachia that has been most affected by the extraction of resources, shifting economic opportunities, and out-migration.[11] Indeed, the inequities in Central Appalachia have been well documented.[12] Individuals living in Central Appalachia report lower levels of educational attainment, higher rates of poverty, poorer health and quality of life, less access to fresh fruits and vegetables, limited access to health care, and higher rates of cancer and chronic disease than those living elsewhere in the country.[13] A lifetime of such inequities results in individuals entering older age in poorer health, with limited access to health care and fewer opportunities for engagement. The out-migration of younger generations from the Central Appalachian region aggravates these challenges.[14]

Beyond the elimination of support that younger generations provide to their families, the elimination of working-aged individuals from the tax base reduces the amount of funding for social services. Across the region, senior centers are closing.[15] Once the central hub of social activity among aging and older adults, many communities are now without one. Services available to the aging population have shrunk over the last twenty years.[16] Access to medical care is now hours away.[17] Very few have access to a geriatrician, instead relying on a combination of emergency rooms and MinuteClinics.[18] While the aging population in Central Appalachia continues to grow, the resources available to them are shrinking at an alarming rate. The results are more individuals entering older adulthood in poor health.

Frank's experience, which opens up this chapter, unfortunately, is far from unique. The realities for aging LGBTQIA+ populations are equally frightening. To date, there has been very little work done examining the health outcomes of aging LGBTQIA+ individuals,[19] but what is known is alarming. Compared to non-LGBTQIA+ individuals, lesbians have higher rates of disability and cardiovascular disease. Gay men have a higher risk of cancer and HIV and are twice as likely to live alone. Transgender individuals report higher rates of discrimination. Bisexual individuals report higher rates of poor mental health.[20] The overlapping maladaptive health outcomes of individuals who identify as LGBTQIA+ are the result of a society that marginalizes this population. The result being a system that prevents LGBTQIA+ individuals from accessing health care, whether due to fear or economic inability. Racial minority aging LGBTQIA+ populations face even worse expressions of these disparities.[21] These challenges can be further exacerbated by geographic location, with rural aging LGBTQIA+ individuals facing the potential for extreme health disparities related to access to care and social support.[22]

LGBTQIA+ Appalachian Identities

Diane and Marlene are movers. Since they have been together, they always have been. Diane (age fifty-six, white, lesbian) has always wanted to move around. In her own words:

> Ya but we were... we... I'd say that's the longest place we've lived in the last how many years is Tennessee. What ten years maybe? 'Cause that's where we were when we got Riley. We were living in Tennessee, so that's where she was adopted at... was Tennessee. But like I've said, we've been together for thirteen years going on fourteen.

Their constant moving has taken a toll on the family's finances, especially for Marlene, who lost her job, in part, she believes due to homophobia. Around the same time, they took in their thirteen-year-old granddaughter. It has reached the point that family members are questioning Diane's mental health and the couple might have to file for bankruptcy.

> Diane: We both have a hard time with that. Bad, 'cause we were in the process of filing for bankruptcy, and we had to stop paying the attorneys, 'cause we had no money to pay em. From moving, yes. 'Cause we moved too much. Ya, it's my fault. Well, my brother was tellin me the other day, he thinks I'm bipolar. They've diagnosed me with major depression, but he thinks I'm bipolar.

> Marlene (age fifty-five, white, lesbian): It... one of the symptoms is... ya, and she does have some ADHD too. Sometimes has trouble concentrating and remembering things and that kind of stuff. 'Cause she takes medications, and plus sometimes I have to remind her to take her medication, 'cause she forgets to take it. And the more pressure she has on her, the worse it gets.

The lack of income has added additional stress for the family of three. In entering what were supposed to be their retirement years, Diane and Marlene find themselves unemployed, raising a grandchild, and unable to access needed mental and physical health resources.[23]

A few counties over, Donna (age fifty-four, white, lesbian) and Vicky (age fifty-five, white, lesbian) live on the side of a small mountain with their five adopted children and their coterie of animals. They are out, proud, and engaged in their school and community through Vicky's job at the local health clinic. When asked about the discrimination they may face, they report none, "And people are saying they're so discriminated against here they've had to move away. And I'm like, yeah, no... I don't... I don't... I don't see that."

Not even two counties over Frank, whose quote opens this chapter, would readily tell anyone who listened not to come out. For Frank, a lifetime of victimization and discrimination has resulted in him trying to hide his identity. He often finds himself as a sort of guide for questioning and other gay individuals, being what he perceived as the only gay male in the county. Although he hated it, he became a begrudging mentor for younger generations.

What connects these stories is the shared experience of aging in rural Central Appalachia. They also highlight a broader reality; there is not one monolithic aging experience in Central Appalachia.

LGBTQIA+ Aging in Appalachia
Identity Concealment
There exists a widespread feeling of discrimination and victimization among aging LGBTQIA+ Appalachians. Discrimination and victimization served as a driver for feelings of exclusion.[24] Pat (age sixty-eight, white, lesbian), a married stepmother of one, described a historically hostile environment faced by gays and lesbians she had experienced her entire life: "[B]ack then it was very hard to become openly gay... especially for women.... We didn't get beat up like [gays] did but we got slandered." The negative experience continues to linger in her memory.

The fear of discrimination often extended beyond the individual to how their family members were perceived in the community. Interactions in school required careful negotiation. The concern was not for themselves but for their children or grandchildren. They were afraid that their children or grandchildren would experience discrimination due to association. While the current fear among many does not seem to be connected necessarily to physical violence, there remains a fear of more subtle discrimination. In the case of Diane (age fifty-six, white, lesbian) and her spouse, Marlene (age fifty-five, white, lesbian), the concern for their grandchild existed despite their differing feelings on disclosure:

> Diane: I was just gonna say, I don't even feel comfortable going to my granddaughter's school... because people look at us funny. We keep to ourselves. We very rarely go anywhere.

Marlene: You know, I went out on a field trip with [granddaughter's] school, because she asked me to go. You know, and everybody was friendly and talked to me and that kind of stuff, you know, but, like I said, they are not real overt about it. They're not like up in your face.

These feelings were verified by actions. People in their community would, at times, try to threaten and scare them. Recalling when he was younger, Frank shared: "People up here would say things. They would attack me. Pull guns on me and throw things. One night I saw someone in white out sneaking behind my house, and [I] pulled out a gun and chased them around a mountain."[25] Frank reported these incidents to his local police department but was not sure that members of the department were not involved. Others shared that often it was too complicated to overcome the existing assumptions around lesbian and gay identity that had permeated their community.[26]

Identity concealment was one common method of attempting to avoid discrimination and challenge assumptions.[27] Due to previous negative interactions with medical professionals who rejected lesbian or gay clients, individuals would withhold their sexual identity. As Babs (age fifty-five, lesbian, white), shared:

We have had difficulty finding a steady medical provider—discrimination might be a very harsh word—but once they found out that I was a lesbian . . . and they found out that my wife was, they treated us completely different and refused to. . . at one point, they refused to let me pick up her medication. They refused to give her information for me. Yeah. It was just very awkward, and the doctor actually, at one point, told me that he did not believe in same-sex relationships.

For Babs and her partner, they felt identity concealment was required in order to seek health care and community resources and to be engaged in the community. Navigating identity concealment and disclosure results in undue stress. It also requires individuals to navigate their multiple competing identities. In Central Appalachia, these competing identities can be challenging due to a more limited geographic and social context. Individuals begin to develop multiple identities among different groups as a means of coping with the desire to be out and the necessity to remain hidden.

Identity concealment can lead to loneliness and social isolation. Loneliness and social isolation have been identified as among the most significant health threats facing the aging population. Loneliness and social isolation are now thought to be a factor in multiple chronic illnesses.[28] The stress of isolation can result in maladaptive health outcomes, both through neurological and biological processes. Social isolation also limits social contact, resulting in limited opportunity to interact with others, to access resources, and to see health care professionals. Isolation and social exclusion were common factors among aging LGBTQIA+ individuals in Central Appalachia. Frank felt that social exclusion was a negative part of gay identity. He shared that:

> They really do need something in places like this, so the younger kids that's gay would have somewhere that they could see that they wasn't in a boat by themselves. Because you feel so by yourself when you come out, you know? You think you're the only one. And then they could see that they... make them feel better about theirself, that they're not in a boat alone.

Heterosexism and Rurality

Assumptions of heterosexuality resulted in feelings of stress and anxiety when meeting with health care providers. Heterosexuality is assumed to be the default orientation. It has shaped the development of the American health care system. Those who do not conform to these heterosexual assumptions can become isolated from the health care system. From the medical forms patients fill out through the wall art hanging in the office to the questions doctors ask—these cultural beliefs about heterosexuality can make individuals feel uneasy and untrusting of the health care system.

Aging LGBTQIA+ individuals experience this heterosexism in the health care system in different ways. Deborah felt that her health care was compromised once her provider found out she was a lesbian, with the provider going as far as to voice his discomfort with same-sex relationships. For Deborah (age fifty-two, white, lesbian), the challenges accessing health care extended from physical to mental health care. Sharing her experience in seeking marriage counseling, she stated:

> She [wife] got very depressed. It caused a lot of trouble in our relationship. We tried to find a therapist to help us through it, and

we had so much difficulty finding a therapist that would counsel same-sex, and then when we did find someone that would counsel, it was still very predominately [a] male/female [viewpoint]. . . . That was very difficult. We actually had to drop out of therapy.

The lack of social services available to rural aging gay and lesbian individuals influences their overall quality of life. As one lesbian couple, who had lost their jobs, explained, even when social services are available, aging LGBTQIA+ individuals may be fearful of accessing them:

I didn't want to take any chances, since they're a Christian organization. . . . The lady offered to pray for us, or with us, and I said, "Yes, absolutely," you know. Cause we identify as Christian . . . but a lot of people think that's an oxymoron around here, that you can't possibly be gay and be a Christian too.

In addition to managing sexual identity in a heterosexist society, aging LGBTQIA+ individuals face the same problems that most rural community members face: problems with access to appropriate care. Dean (age fifty-two, gay, white) was slowly recovering from a small stroke that was exacerbated by his inability to access care quickly. Similarly, Dean's friend Tim (age sixty-two, gay, white) had recently decided to stop seeking care in his hometown. It was particularly hard for Tim to come to this conclusion; several physician errors resulting in surgery led him to believe that care in another environment would be more appropriate.

It was common to talk about the lack of accessible health services and the requirements for accessing health services. In one case, Randall (age sixty-two, white, gay) was fearful after an accident about the affect a lack of medical professionals would have on his long-term care. He stated, "There was a period of time when it first started really going downhill that I thought I was going to be using a walker and that kind of thing, but now I do pretty well day to day." Frank (age fifty-seven, gay) faced challenges in locating doctors. He stated, "Well, where I'm on disability, they got the few ones that'll take the medical card. And that kind of shuts you down. And we ain't got that much here. We ain't got much of nothing, you know?" Others, such as Tim (age sixty-two, gay) were blunter, stating that, "Well. . . services, yes, there's like. . . nothing."

Sexual identity played a role in health care interactions. Although understanding a patient's sexual identity should be considered part of the ordinary course of treatment, from experience, it is far from the norm. Henry (age sixty-seven, gay), felt that sexual identity should be part of the conversation with health care professionals, but that it was often overlooked:

> I don't know if it's because of the HIPAA laws or… I'm really not sure. Sometimes I think they kind of skirt around it and don't directly approach it, but they kind of skirt around it and ask questions that… you know what they're trying to get at, but they just don't come right out and ask.

Henry's comments highlight an uneasy tension. Many aging LGBTQIA+ individuals feel that sexual identity should be addressed as part of routine care. At the same time, some were willing to identify barriers for providers: in this case, falsely attributing HIPAA to the lack of inquiry. Some, such as Vicki (age fifty-five, white, lesbian) felt it was important for their doctor to discuss sexual identity but that it was not necessarily the most crucial aspect of the visit. She stated, "Right, yeah… it's like are you afraid to disclose your orientation? I'm not really afraid, but it's just… it's none of their business. You know what I mean?" In this instance, Vicki recognizes the importance and states that she would not be afraid to disclose, but also that she would not go out of her way to inform. Vicki worked at a health care clinic, the only major one in the area. Her thoughts are shaped by what she sees day in and day out in delivering care to a poorer, more vulnerable population. In her mind, other factors are more important than sexual identity when delivering health care.

Navigating Identity in Appalachia

> And I do love my neighbors. They drive me nuts with their narrow-mindedness and their whatever, but I'm still trying to broaden their horizons.
>
> —Hillary (age seventy, lesbian, white).

Overall, these stories highlight the complexities in navigating life as an aging LGBTQIA+ individual living in Central Appalachia. Yet what binds everyone who spoke to us together is a shared love of their community. These experiences are only a small glimpse into the lives of rural aging Appalachian gay and lesbian individuals. They point to the complexity of what it means to age as a rural gay or lesbian individual. They highlight the divide in experiences that geographically close individuals may feel when belonging to a marginalized community. There are, however, shared experiences around access to care, feelings of community, social isolation, and victimization. The aging Appalachian LGBTQIA+ population has developed a resilience that assisted them in navigating a complex sociopolitical environment that both challenged and negatively impacted their overall well-being and health.

The stories also point to the reality that living and aging in Central Appalachia is not a monolithic experience for anyone. They point to the infinite diversity that exists within the region. They highlight the fact that for marginalized groups, their experiences are not uniform. The belief that Appalachians share the same cultural beliefs extends to an assumption any marginalized groups would have the same experiences. Aging LGBTQIA+ Appalachians share a common Appalachian identity, but their experiences are different. For some, the region has provided them a place to live and age with limited negative impact. Others share the belief that living in Appalachia has resulted in a life of fear, discrimination, and poor health. The limited opportunities of the region or their strong connection to home have prevented them from leaving. While they may identify with the region, they are unable to fully reconcile the ways it has affected them. It is the dichotomy of their experiences in the region and their feelings for the region that create internal conflict. While many readily accept their Appalachian identity, they also want to be able to equally express their LGBTQIA+ identity. Some, such as Donna and Vicki, have been able to reconcile these identities. Others like Frank still struggle with the belief that his LGBTQIA+ identity and his Appalachian identity cannot coexist.

Moving forward, work is needed to fully embrace aging LGBTQIA+ members as part of the LGBTQIA+ Appalachian community.[29] It must be recognized that they exist. They must be engaged. At the same time, there needs be consideration of how to best to engage and recognize the lived experiences of these trailblazers. Yes, many remain hidden—some purposefully so—but recognizing that this community exists and identifying ways to engage with it will add depth to current LGBTQIA+ movements through understanding the history of LGBTQIA+ Appalachians and LGBTQIA+ Appalachia. Doing so will mean challenging existing notions of what constitutes Appalachia and who lives in the region. It will require further embracing the diversity of the region. It will require the urban-centered LGBTQIA+ organization and cultural systems to extend their reach. As an LGBTQIA+ individual, these challenges are further exacerbated.

The challenges of health care access, social support, and economic viability that exist for all aging Appalachians exist for the aging LGBTQIA+ population as well. The aging LGBTQIA+ population faces additional barriers to accessing care and support. Health care providers must recognize the systemic institutional and cultural factors that discourage LGBTQIA+ Appalachians from accessing care. They must commit themselves to delivering affirming care. They must uphold their oaths to treat—few providers would deny a heterosexual partner the right to assist in care, so why is it acceptable for same-sex partners to be denied this right? Social systems, such as senior centers and community outreach groups, must work just as hard to ensure that their services are accessible and welcoming to all. These programmatic enterprises should reach out and engage the aging LGBTQIA+ population to understand their needs. Both groups must work diligently to remove heterosexist bias from their practices. Through these activities, as well as other economic interventions, it will become possible for aging LGBTQIA+ Appalachians to better integrate within their communities and to increase their access to viable health care, support, and economic development.

Work must continue to further recognize and engage with this population, particularly as more and more of their rights are being stripped away. It is only through engagement with this population and recognizing that LGBTQIA+ identities exist across the life span that we can create a more equitable society—a society that engages all and recognizes the multiple, and often competing, expressions of identity.

NOTES

1   All names are pseudonyms.

2   Jennifer M. Ortman, Victoria A. Velkoff, and Howard Hogan, "An Aging Nation: The Older Population in the United States," United States Census Bureau, May 2014.

3   Karen I. Fredriksen-Goldsen, Hyun-Jun Kim, Amanda A.E. Bryan, Chengshi Shiu, and Charles E. Emlet, "The Cascading Effects of Marginalization and Pathways of Resilience in Attaining Good Health Among LGBT Older Adults," *Gerontologist* 57(suppl 1) (February 2017), S72–S83.

4   Soon Kyu Choi and Ilan H. Meyer, *LGBT Aging: A Review of Research Findings, Needs, and Policy Implications*, Williams Institute, UCLA School of Law, 2017.

5   Kevin J. Bennett, Tyrone F. Borders, George M. Holmes, Katy Backes Kozhimannil, and Erika Ziller, "What Is Rural? Challenges and Implications of Definitions That Inadequately Encompass Rural People and Places," *Health Affairs* 38, no. 12 (December 2019): 1985–92.

6   Mary L. Gray, *Out in the Country: Youth, Media, and Queer Visibility in Rural America* (New York: New York University Press, 2019).

7   The multiple research studies were approved by the University of Kentucky IRB; multiple funders supported this fieldwork, including the University of Kentucky Office of LGBTQ* Resources, the University of Kentucky Appalachian Center, the University of Kentucky College of Medicine, the OLLI Donovan Endowment Fund, and JustFundKY.

8   Barbara Ellen Smith, "The Place of Appalachia," *Journal of Appalachian Studies* 8, no. 1 (Spring 2002): 42–49.

9   Ronald D. Eller, *Uneven Ground: Appalachia since 1945* (Lexington: University Press of Kentucky, 2009).

10   Elizabeth Catte, *What You Are Getting Wrong about Appalachia* (Cleveland: Belt Publishing, 2018).

11   Ibid.

12   Keith J. Zullig and Michael Hendryx, "Health-Related Quality of Life among Central Appalachian Residents in Mountaintop Mining Counties," *American Journal of Public Health* 101, no. 5 (May 2011): 848–53.

13   Nancy E. Schoenberg, Harry E. Bundy, Jordan A. Baeker Bispo, Christina R. Studts, Brent T. Shelton, and Neil Fields, "A Rural Appalachian Faith-Placed Smoking Cessation Intervention," *Journal of Religion and Health* 54, no. 2 (April 2015): 598–611.

14   Robert L. Ludke and Phillip J. Obermiller, "Recent Trends in Appalachian Migration, 2005–2009," *Journal of Appalachian Studies* 20, no. 1 (Spring 2014): 24–42.

15   Joshua M. Wiener, Michael Lepore, and Jessica Jones, "What Policymakers Need to Know about Long-Term Services and Supports," *Public Policy & Aging Report* 28, no. 1 (2018): 29–34.

16   Graham D. Rowles, "What's Rural about Rural Aging? An Appalachian Perspective*," *Journal of Rural Studies* 4, no. 2 (1988): 115–24.

17   Janice Probst, Jan Marie Eberth, and Elizabeth Crouch, "Structural Urbanism Contributes to Poorer Health Outcomes for Rural America," *Health Affairs* 38, no. 12 (December 2019): 1976–84.

18   Hayley Drew Germack, Ryan Kandrack, and Grant R. Martsolf, "When Rural Hospitals Close, the Physician Workforce Goes," *Health Affairs* 38, no. 12 (December 2019): 2086–94.

19   Karen I. Fredriksen-Goldsen and Hyun-Jun Kim, "The Science of Conducting Research with LGBT Older Adults—An Introduction to Aging with Pride: National Health, Aging, and Sexuality/Gender Study (NHAS)," *Gerontologist* 57(suppl 1) (February 2017): S1–S14.

20   Karen I. Fredriksen-Goldsen, "Dismantling the Silence: LGBTQ Aging Emerging from the Margins," *Gerontologist* 57, no. 1 (2017): 121–28.

21   Karen I. Fredriksen-Goldsen, Charles P. Hoy-Ellis, Jayn Goldsen, Charles A. Emlet, and Nancy R. Hooyman, "Creating a Vision for the Future: Key Competencies and Strategies for Culturally Competent Practice with Lesbian, Gay, Bisexual, and Transgender (LGBT) Older Adults in the Health and Human Services," *Journal Gerontolological Social Work* 57, no. 2–4 (2014): 80–107.

22   Sandra S. Butler, "LGBT Aging in the Rural Context," *Annual Review of Gerontology & Geriatrics* 37, no. 1 (January 2017): 127–42.

23   Rates of grandparents raising grandchildren have climbed since the mid-2010s, in part driven by the opioid epidemic. Central Appalachia has some of the highest rates of grandparents raising grandchildren, or grandfamilies; see "The Opioid Crisis and Grandparents Raising Grandchildren," United States Census Bureau, April 22, 2019, accessed October 6, 2021, https://www.census.gov/library/stories/2019/04/opioid-crisis-grandparents-raising-grandchildren.html.

24   Gordon Allport, *The Nature of Prejudice*, 25th anniversary edition (New York: Basic Books, 1979 [1954]).

25   Referring to the Ku Klux Klan.

26   Some may wonder why Frank did not leave this environment. The realities of economics, career prospects, and access to capital to make such a move limits the potential to leave. Cultural and emotional ties to the land and community also affect individuals' decisions.

27   I opt to use the term "identity concealment" for two reasons. First, a closet is for clothes. Second, and perhaps more important, "identity concealment" captures the point that individuals are hiding who they identify as due to the fear of persecution.

28   John T. Cacioppo, Louise C. Hawkley, Greg J. Normam, and Gary G. Bernston, "Social Isolation," *Annals of the New York Academy of Sciences* 123, no. 1 (August 2011): 17–22.

29   Current terminology, such as that of "queer" Appalachia may be off-putting as many associate "queer" with a pejorative leveled against them throughout their lives.

ABOUT THE AUTHOR

Aaron Guest, PhD, MPH, MSW, is a socio-environmental gerontologist and assistant professor of aging at Arizona State University. His primary research line focuses on the social experiences of marginalized aging individuals in rural environments and nonurban centers with a particular interest in working with sexual, racial, and gender minority groups to reduce isolation and health inequalities. He seeks to develop tailored community-based approaches that can be utilized to increase diffusion and translation of health care innovations and, thus, increase access and utilization of critical health programs and services for older adults. Guest grew up in rural South Carolina and completed his PhD in Gerontology at the University of Kentucky, focusing on rural Appalachian lesbian and gay individuals' experiences. He currently lives in Phoenix, Arizona, with his three cats and remains active in Appalachian scholarship and service.

An Appalachian Crip/Queer Environmental Engagement

Rebecca-Eli Long

> I want us to respect and embrace the bodies disabled through environmental destruction, age, war, genocide, abysmal working conditions, hunger, poverty, and twists of fate, rather than deeming them abnormal bodies to isolate, fear, hate, and dispose of. How can bodily and ecological loss become an integral conundrum of both the human and non-human world, accepted in a variety of ways, cure and restoration only a single response among many?
>
> —Eli Clare, "Notes on Natural Worlds, Disabled Bodies, and a Politics of Cure.[1]

Introduction

Eli Clare, a trans disabled writer who grew up in rural working-class Oregon, writes about the complex relation between bodies and environments, especially those that are thought to be somehow abnormal or damaged. While not explicitly about Appalachia, there is much in Clare's analysis that is relevant to understanding queerness in peripheral, out of the way places. This understanding of queerness moves beyond the umbrella of queer identities to think about how divisions are created between the normal and the abnormal, especially when it comes to disabled bodies—which are abnormal and also inherently queer. I also seek to queer the relationship between people and environment, contesting the categories of "natural" and "cultural." Clare's quote above blurs divisions between the person and the environment by drawing parallels between "damage" to the person and environmental harm. These points suggest that disability is important to queerness, which can help us expand queer-Appalachian projects.

In this chapter I examine "crip/queer" theory to better understand how disability justice might build upon and strengthen existing LGBTQIA2S+ movements in Appalachia.[2] "Crip," shorthand for cripple, has been paired with queer to recognize the ways these concepts challenge what is thought of as a good or normal body. Building from this understanding I bring this crip/queer attention to Appalachian landscapes, recognizing the importance of place and environment in Appalachian Studies. By emphasizing the relationships between people and place, I can emphasize how Appalachia's history of extractive industries has harmed the land and people. I suggest a new alliance: a crip/queer environmental engagement that expands the work of queer and environmental activists to critically consider the ways in which these movements can consider disability in conversations about harm and justice. While I argue for the importance of addressing environmental injustice, I firmly believe that disabled people need to be understood as more than just an unfortunate by-product of environmental destruction.

The term "queer" points us toward potential futures.[3] As Appalachia reckons with its relationship with extractive industries, policymakers and developers have spent much time and energy considering what a good future for the region might look like—a region that has often been understood as culturally backward and stuck in the past.[4] When discussing futures for Appalachia, disability is disavowed and the value of a future without disabled people goes uncontested. As Alison Kafer, a leading scholar on the relationship between the crip and the queer argues, "rather than assume that a 'good' future naturally and obviously depends upon the eradication of disability, we must recognize this perspective as colored by histories of ableism and disability oppression."[5] A good future for Appalachia might not be one without experiences of disability but instead one that challenges histories of disability stigma.

Disability stigma runs deep in Appalachia, in no small part due to the stereotypes of the region as backward and dependent—essentially itself disabled. Appalachia's position as America's "Other" has been associated with physical and mental differences in Appalachia's population. Early writing about Appalachia posited that the first European settlers were criminally inclined Anglo-Saxons, and that the isolated landscape led to intermarriage and a prevalence of negative genetic traits.[6] Appalachian people were cast as physically different and often culturally deficient, in need of outside help and development.[7] Through this process, Appalachia becomes a space set apart from the rest of the nation, America's "Other," a frequent source of environmental resources, termed the nation's "sacrifice zone."[8] This othering has exacerbated economic and cultural marginalization, as well as the perceived and actual experience of disability.

This stigma has been used to disempower those who fail to meet capitalist standards of productivity and seek disability assistance through government support.[9] Securing disability benefits in Appalachia is described as "emotionally fraught" and "bound up with self-image," making it difficult to engage with disability outside of stigma and bureaucratic processes.[10] The complex government processes and social judgement that hypothetically weed out the fraudulent claims from those of the "deserving poor" do a poor job of meeting needs and works to marginalize already oppressed communities. We need a more radical way to address disability in our communities, so I turn to crip/queer theory as a potential locus for imagining new futures for Appalachia—futures that radically include different ways of being, while challenging national stereotypes of the region.

Crip/Queer Appalachia

Attitudes toward one's disability can be complex, especially in areas where disability is a result of violence or destruction. Views of disability are also complicated when disability is seen as endemic to a population, as it is in Appalachia. While Disability Studies scholar Tobin Siebers notes that many disabled people do not see their disability as a "flaw" or "defect," are comfortable with who they are, and opt not to seek a cure, they may not necessarily welcome further disablement.[11] Some disabled people may come to claim "crip" identity—a radical repositioning of disability as a form of pride. "Crip" can be understood alongside "queer" as a way of challenging social norms about what a good body and mind might look like. This is especially salient in Appalachia, a region whose othering has been furthered through the othering of its environment and those who live in it.[12]

"Crip" "signals in-group status and solidarity and is intended to deflate mainstream labels such as 'handi-capable,' and 'physically challenged,' terms many activists find patronizing and politically misleading."[13] Like "queer," "crip" is a reclaimed pejorative that has come to be used as a celebration of deviant identity. "Crip" "is a term which has much currency in disability activism and culture but still might seem harsh to those outside those communities."[14] "Crip" primarily entered the academic lexicon of Disability Studies through Carrie Sandahl's 2003 article, "Queering the Crip or Cripping the Queer," Robert McRuer's 2006 *Crip Theory*, and Alison Kafer's 2013 *Feminist Crip Queer*.[15] These keystone texts make intellectual connections between disability and Queer Studies and think about the ways in which intersectionality and solidarity can be performed, both between academic disciplines and individual identities. The phrasing of "crip"/"queer" draws attention to reclaimed radical identities that have the power to transform social relationships.[16]

My turn to the crip/queer has been informed by the rise of Queer Appalachia (@QueerAppalachia) as a social media and cultural movement, highlighting the often rural nature of Appalachian queerness, along with growing collection of work challenging stereotypes of Appalachia as backward and hostile to difference.[17] Queer-Appalachian spaces can exist through academic texts but also reach outside of boundaries to include popular culture, as well as art installations, zines, podcasts, and other multimedia projects. These efforts are not only about "queers," they also work "to queer" how Appalachia is understood and engaged with in new and diverse ways that reach beyond a queer-identified community.

Disability issues crop up throughout *Electric Dirt*, a zine published by Queer Appalachia.[18] Shoog McDaniel writes about the shame of being disabled and superfat and the accompanying frequent exclusion from queer spaces.[19] Another anonymous contributor writes about how having an invisible disability, and how their family and community sees them as a burden.[20] Both these essays grapple with ableism, both internal and external—but neither asks for a cure for their disability, instead focusing on the societal barriers that challenge disabled existence, especially in the rural Appalachian South.

This emphasis on societal barriers and not medicalized impairments is part of what is known as the social model of disability. Popularized by disabled activists to emphasize how they were disabled by attitudes and the environment around them, the social model of disability moves the "problem" of disability from the individual to society. While the social model makes an invaluable theoretical contribution to Disability Studies, it does not always account for the "unhealthy disabled,"[21] a category which can include those living with chronic pain, environmental injury, and other illnesses. These may be amplified but not entirely explained by societal barriers. The role of the environment in disability has been not thoroughly studied, with the social model of disability placing emphasis more on the "built" environment than the "natural" environment.[22] Yet such a divide between built and natural, or between natural and cultural, may limit how we understand disability, especially in queer ways.

Transforming Environmental Politics

Disability can be a result of chance, but it often results from violence, war, poverty, and pollution. Disability may stem from injustice, but it is not itself injustice. To equate disability with suffering is to ignore the value of disability, disabled people, and disability culture. Clare suggests some of the ways in which disabled bodies become used as cautionary tales, rhetorical props: "arguments against drunk driving, drug use, air pollution, lead paint, asbestos, vaccines, and on and on. So many public campaigns use the cultural fear and hatred of disability to make the case against environmental degradation."[23] These arguments reflect the rampant societal ableism that would eugenically seek to prevent disability. The question that arises from Clare's conversation is deeply impactful: "How do we witness, name, and resist the injustices that reshape and damage all kinds of body-minds—plant and animal, organic and inorganic, nonhuman and human—while not equating disability with injustice?"[24] Multi-issue organizing requires engaging with disability beyond just an unfortunate event but as an often queer way of being in the world.

Many of our movements, those that developed both inside and outside the region, argue against disability and disabled existence. For example, in Minden, West Virginia, an old coal-mining town, residents disproportionately experience cancer as a result of the land being poisoned with toxic chemicals disposed in an old mine site.[25] In Martin County, Kentucky, residents faced decades of unsafe drinking water, and now many struggle to pay their water bills.[26] A recent spike in black lung cases in the region has also brought miners together to help each other with disability benefits paperwork.[27] These issues fall outside the boundaries of what some would consider disability issues, a category that might be more likely to evoke those with congenital disabilities than disabilities acquired from living in damaged landscapes. Such cases queer how disability can be understood, and they also expand on the ways we can think about queerness.

We should fight against extraction and exploitation, but we must also think more carefully about how we use disabled bodies to further such arguments and how these arguments leverage disability stigma. A crip/queer environmental politics recognizes this often unconscious ableism and seeks to address the shortcomings in mainstream sustainable development and related movements where this ableism is rampant. A crip/queer environmental engagement can challenge the ways in which we think of bodies in relation to the so-called natural world. Sustainable development fails to challenge entrenched systems in the radical ways demanded by crip/queer projects. In fact, mainstream sustainable development "has not been very radical" and "has sought to refocus existing development initiatives and policy action rather than transform their principles or practice."[28]

Environmentalism, and even the more intersectional environmental justice movement, fail to sufficiently address ableism. Feminist scholar-activist Valerie Ann Johnson wrote that the environmental justice movement typically addresses disparities across race, ethnicity, and socioeconomic status but doesn't consider gender, sexuality, and disability.[29] Echoing some of the concerns of Clare, Johnson asks, "When [environmental] harm occurs, do the people harmed become disabled in a way that renders them less capable of active participation in the movement work?"[30] Disabled people should be seen as bringing a valuable perspective to all our movements, working to address broad, multi-issue concerns.

This is not simply a failure of inclusion. I contend that disabled people are situated to provide valuable knowledge in the "arts of living on a damaged planet," a way of thinking relationally with the multispecies damage wrought by human overdevelopment.[31] For example, those with environmental and chemical sensitivities are familiar with techniques to mitigate the effects of inhaling wildfire smoke.[32] Yet these skills alone are not enough to save disabled people in the face of increased environment destruction. Disabled people are often disproportionately impacted by climate change and resulting natural disasters.[33] In particular, this issue intersects with race and class and requires multi-issue solidarity to address. Disabled people are both more likely to be exposed to environmental disaster and are more vulnerable to the effects of these disasters when they do occur.[34]

In an essay, Disability Justice founder Patty Berne writes:

Let's start by openly, joyously proclaiming that we [queer and trans disabled people] are natural beings, not aberrations of nature.... When we begin to see the planet through this lens [of queer ecology], we remember that the entire world has biodiversity that is precious, necessary for our survival, and deeply threated. Whether we're looking at ecology, society, or our human culture, diversity is our best defense against the threats of climate change.[35]

From Berne's standpoint queer and disabled people are an essential part of human diversity. More than just diversity, we bring essential knowledge that can help imagine new queer-Appalachian futures.

Placing Disability in Appalachia

In addressing the relevance of the crip/queer to Appalachia, it is necessary to consider the centrality of place and environment in Appalachian Studies. Appalachia has long been constructed as a place apart from the rest America. Appalachian Studies scholar William Schumann notes that "Appalachian place-making is often dominated by powerful economic and political actors, such as energy companies and elected officials, who define resource exploitation as a way of ensuring regional economic development and the national security of the United States."[36] External interests have shaped what we think of as Appalachia.

Likewise, there have been local, parallel strands of place-making that focus on resistance to extractive industries and progressive social movements. Thus, "place-making in Appalachia operates on the principle of marking difference between one reading of human-environmental relations and all others."[37] As Steven Fisher and Barbara Ellen Smith argue, "place" has the potential to contribute to "new forms of progressive organizing."[38]

The people and regions that are cast as "disabled" are a result of power dynamics and socially constructed ideals of normalcy. Rather than being a medical fact, what is considered as disabled is rooted in histories of ableism, disability stigma, and oppression. The perception of Appalachia as a disabled region, as well as a region with a high statistical prevalence of disability, can be read as a result of the region's positioning as a periphery.[39] In Appalachia, disability is often associated with histories of capitalism and environmental extraction, which profoundly impacts both human and nonhuman health and functioning. Large-scale timber industries created the risk for occupational injury.[40] Coal mining caused, and continues to cause, a condition called black lung, which severely impacts human health at the same time as it damages the environment. More recently, struggles against pipelines, such as the Mountain Valley Pipeline, have raised concerns about the safety and well-being on both a community and environmental level.

The study of queer ecologies challenges normative conceptions of nature as a space separate from human culture and considers nature spaces to have been constructed historically around ideas of cisheteronormativity.[41] Queering nature and ecology allows for new ways of thinking through human and nonhuman relationships. While "queer ecology" draws upon the relations of queer-identified people and the natural world, we can consider the term more broadly in the sense of unusual alliances and places that defy easy categorization—for example, Appalachia.[42]

I turn to the phrase "assemblage" to describe the complex relationships that form on multiple scales between organisms of various types. Anna Tsing writes:

> Ecologists turned to assemblages to get around the sometimes fixed and bounded connotations of ecological 'community.' . . . Assemblages are open-ended gatherings. They allow us to ask about communal effects without assuming them. They show us potential histories in the making If history without progress is indeterminate and multidirectional, might assemblages show us its possibilities?[43]

Assemblages allow for a relational understanding that recognizes how our social world is enacted by both human and nonhuman actors. Understanding this complexity lets us further think about how the assemblage that makes up the environmental movement can be cripped and queered. Assemblages move beyond intersectionality and a focus on identity to think about multiple forces that destabilized fixed categories and identities.

Environmental issues can also be disability issues, which can also be race and class issues. If Appalachia, perhaps, is a queer place, these issues are also implicated in queer movements. McDaniel provides some ways this might look for radical queer organizing:

List accessibility on your events. Ask your friends about what they need help with and try to make time to help out those folks who need a little more. Plan trips that are specifically accessible and fun for your friends who might not get invited much. Talk to your friends who say or do ablest [*sic*] things. Don't talk about your diet with us; we don't care.[44]

Building anti-ableist practices into community organizing creates a meaningful way to address disability histories in Appalachia. Disability has been part of negative stereotypes about Appalachia, but it needs to be addressed as a very real part of our communities and movements in ways that challenge ableism.

Central Appalachia has become an environment that is both disabled and disabling, where human disability exists in relation to and as a result of environmental damage. Seeing disability as an ecological process shows the ways in which experiences of disability are implicated in environmental movements. By using queer frameworks, I understand these not as two separate phenomena but as a result of the interactions between nature and culture. The environment of Appalachia has been shaped by extractive industry, which has created both harm to the environment and the beings who live with this land.

Conclusion

Though these issues are theoretical, they are also highly practical and provide an urgently needed critique. Disabled lives are some of the most precarious lives in this age of "Trump country," a phrase that stigmatizes Appalachia at the same time as it threatens both queer and disability communities. The critical Disability Studies method of tracing ableism shows the devaluing of entire populations rampant in today's political landscape. Ableism compounds the racism and xenophobia against migrants at the border. Ableism feeds white supremacy and white nationalism. Ableism feeds the stigmatization of queerness as disease. Disabled migrants, people of color, and queer people are all more likely to have their existence invalidated—which is why claiming cross-movement solidarity is of the utmost importance.

In this conclusion, I briefly consider the disability justice movement and how it is helpful in building our movements here in Appalachia. Disability justice as a movement was started by a group of disability activists who were multiply marginalized.[45] Disability justice goes beyond notions of rights and seeks to center the voices of those who are marginalized in traditional disability rights spaces, such as queer people, Indigenous people, and people of color. Disability justice recognizes that rights are granted by a settler-colonialist cisheteropatriarchal state that many are unable to access. The disability justice approach is an intersectional one, and it argues for leadership by those most impacted, and, thus, is helpful in thinking about those who are marginalized by ability, gender, sexuality, class, and geography.

Disability justice is not a panacea, but it has the potential to go a great way toward building cross-issue movements that address the interrelations of embodied experiences and the larger power imbalances that have had real impacts on the region. Though scholarship and activism do not always neatly align, all of the fields addressed in this article have scholar-activist roots and often blur the boundaries of theory and praxis. While fighting against extractive capitalist forces that have caused great damage, can we engage with disability as more than just a byproduct of environmental harm? Can we recognize the battles that disabled people have fought, both inside and outside of Appalachia, to prove the value of our lives? Can we recognize that a post-coal future does not need to eliminate disability and acknowledge the relational aspects of disablement between human and nonhuman systems?

This chapter introduced the phrase *crip/queer environmental engagement* and used it to think about the positioning of disabled people as props in arguments for environmental well-being. In doing this, I explicitly affirm the value of disabled lives. This is a radical positioning of disability that resists statements such as, "disabled lives have value, but wouldn't it be better if no one was disabled?" Through the use of Disability Studies scholars, many of whom are disabled themselves, I resist the idea that that a good future hinges on the eradication of disability. In fact, I contend that disability is a valuable part of the human experience with a disruptive potential that is similar, though not identical to, queerness.

By bringing crip and queer together theoretically I think about how our attempts to queer Appalachia need to also include understandings of disability. Throughout this chapter, I "claim disability" as an analytic to encourage cross-movement solidarity.[46] As Simi Linton writes, "The material that binds us [disabled people] is the art of finding one another, of identifying and naming disability in a world reluctant to discuss it, and of unearthing historically and culturally significant material that relates to our experience."[47] Bringing disability into our conversations is an important political act that can enhance our conversations of sustainability and environmental justice. A "good future" may not equal the absence of disability—as the biomedical model might suggest—but, rather, a reinvention of disability's social significance and cultural possibilities as part of our understanding of a queer Appalachia.

NOTES

1   Eli Clare, "Notes on Natural Worlds, Disabled Bodies, and a Politics of Cure," in *Disability Studies and the Environmental Humanities: Toward an Eco-Crip Theory*, edited by Sarah Jaquette Ray and Jay Sibara (Lincoln: University of Nebraska Press, 2017), 255.

2   Referring to lesbian, gay, bisexual, transgender, queer, intersex, asexual, and two spirit, this acronym acknowledges a range of sexuality and genders that challenge cisheteronormativity, including that of Indigenous communities.

3   José Esteban Muñoz, *Cruising Utopia: The Then and There of Queer Futurity* (New York: New York University Press, 2009).

4   Jack E. Weller, *Yesterday's People: Life in Contemporary Appalachia* (Lexington: University Press of Kentucky, 1993).

5   Alison Kafer, *Feminist Queer Crip* (Bloomington: Indiana University Press, 2013), 3.

6   Harry Caudill, *Night Comes to the Cumberlands: A Biography of a Depressed Area* (Boston: Little, Brown, 1962); Jack Weller, *Yesterday's People: Life in Comtempory Appalchia* (Lexington: University Press of Kentucky, 1965).

7   Henry D. Shapiro, *Appalachia on Our Mind: The Southern Mountains and Mountaineers in American Consciousness 1870–1920* (Chapel Hill: University of North Carolina Press, 1986).

8   Julia Fox, "Mountaintop Removal in West Virginia: An Environmental Sacrifice Zone," *Organization and Environment* 12, no. 2 (June 1999): 163–83.

9   Colin Barnes and Geof Mercer, "Disability, Work, and Welfare: Challenging the Social Exclusion of Disabled People" *Work, Employment, and Society* 19, no. 3 (September 2005): 527–45.

10 Rob Spirko, "In Appalachia, Disability Stigma Has Dangerous Effects," *Rooted in Rights*, September 21, 2018, accessed October 7, 2021, https://rootedinrights.org/in-appalachia-disability-stigma-has-dangerous-effects.

11 Tobin Siebers, *Disability Theory* (Ann Arbor: University of Michigan Press, 2008), 4.

12 Rebecca R. Scott, *Removing Mountains: Extracting Nature and Identity in the Appalachian Coalfields* (Minneapolis: University of Minnesota Press, 2010).

13 Victoria Ann Lewis, "Crip," in *Keywords for Disability Studies*, edited by Rachel Adams, Benjamin Reiss, and David Serlin (New York: New York University Press, 2015).

14   Kafer, *Feminist Queer Crip*, 15.

15   Carrie Sandahl, "Queering the Crip or Cripping The Queer? Intersections of Queer and Crip Identities in Solo Autobiographical Performance," *GLQ: A Journal of Lesbian and Gay Studies* 9, nos. 1–2 (April 2003): 25–56; Robert McRuer, *Crip Theory: Cultural Signs of Queerness and Disability* (New York: New York University Press, 2006); Kafer, *Feminist Queer Crip*.

16   My understanding of "crip/queer" and its implications has been influenced by Sami Schalk, "Coming to Claim Crip: Disidentification with/in Disability Studies," *Disability Studies Quarterly* 33, no. 2 (March 2013).

17   See, e.g., Darci McFarland, ed., *Bible Belt Queers* (self-published, 2019); Hillery Glasby, Sherrie Gradin, and Rachael Ryerson, eds., *Storytelling in Queer Appalachia: Imagining and Writing the Unspeakable Other* (Morgantown: West Virginia University Press, 2020); Rachel Garringer's "Country Queers" (oral history project and podcast), accessed October 7, 2021, https://countryqueers. com.

18   Queer Appalachia, ed., *Electric Dirt: A Celebration of Queer Voices and Identities in Appalachia and the South*, vol. 1 (Bluefield, WV: Queer Appalachia, 2017); Brontez Purnell, ed., *Electric Dirt: A Celebration of Queer Voices and Identities from Appalachia and the South*, vol. 2 (Bluefield, WV: Queer Appalachia, 2020).

19   Shoog McDaniel (Instagram: @Shooglet), "Queer Rural Disabled," in *Electric Dirt*, vol. 1, 152–53.

20   Anonymous, Untitled, in *Electric Dirt*, vol. 1, 154–60.

21   Susan Wendell, "Unhealthy Disabled: Treating Chronic Illnesses as Disabilities," *Hypatia* 16, no. 4 (Fall 2001): 17–33.

22   Kafer, *Feminist Crip Queer*, 129.

23   Clare, "Notes on Natural Worlds," 251–52.

24   Ibid.

25   Natalie Baptiste, "This Town Is So Toxic, They Want It Wiped Off the Map," *Mother Jones*, January 8, 2018, accessed October 7, 2021, https://www.motherjones.com/ environment/2018/01/this-town-is-so-toxic-they-want-it-wiped-off-the-map.

26   Sydney Boyles, "First These Kentuckians Couldn't Drink the Water. Now they Can't Afford It," NPR, October 31, 2019, accessed October 7, 2021, https://tinyurl. com/ktyhwbkr.

27   Carrie Arnold, "A Scourge Returns: Black Lung in Appalachia," *Environmental Health Perspectives* 124, no. 1 (December 2015): A13–18.

28   W.M. Adams, *Green Development: Environment and Sustainability in a Developing World* (Routledge: New York, 2009), 116.

29   Valerie Ann Johnston, "Bringing Together Feminist Disability Studies and Environmental Justice," in *Disability Studies and the Environmental Humanities: Toward an Eco-Crip Theory*, eds. Sarah Jaquette Ray and Jay Sibara (Lincoln: University of Nebraska Press, 2017), 73–93.

30   Ibid, 85.

31   Anna Lowenhaupt Tsing, Heather Anne Swanson, Elaine Gan, and Nils Bubandt, eds., *Arts of Living on a Damaged Planet: Ghosts and Monsters of the Anthropocene* (Minneapolis: University of Minnesota Press, 2017).

32   Leah Lakshmi Piepzna-Samarasinha, *Care Work: Dreaming Disability Justice* (Vancouver, BC: Arsenal Pulp Press, 2018), 40.

33   United Nations, "How Climate Change Disproportionately Impacts Those with Disabilities," accessed October 7, 2021, https://tinyurl.com/223mby5d.

34   Catherine Jampel, "Intersections of Disability Justice, Racial Justice and Environmental Justice," *Environmental Sociology* 1, no. 4 (2018), accessed October 7, 2021, https://par.nsf.gov/servlets/purl/10058562.

35   Patty Berne, with Vanessa Raditz, "To Survive Climate Catastrophe, Look to Queer and Disabled Folks," in *Disability Visibility*, ed. Alice Wong (New York: Vintage, 2020), 233.

36   William Schumann, "Introduction," in *Appalachia Revisited: New Perspectives on Place, Tradition, and Progress*, eds. William Schumann and Rebecca Adkins Fletcher (Lexington: University of Kentucky, 2016), 9.

37   Ibid.

38   Stephen L. Fisher and Barbara Ellen Smith, "Introduction," in *Transforming Places: Lessons from Appalachia*, ed. Stephen L. Fisher and Barbara Ellen Smith (Urbana: University of Illinois Press, 2012), 6.

39   John L. McCoy, Miles Davis, and Russell E. Hudson, "Geographic Patterns of Disability in the United States," *Social Security Bulletin* 57, no. 1 (Spring 1994): 25; Kathy A. Ruffing, "Geographic Pattern of Disability Receipt Largely Reflects Economic and Demographic Factors," Center on Budget and Policy Priorities, January 9, 2015, accessed October 7, 2021, https://www.cbpp.org/sites/default/files/atoms/files/1-8-15ss.pdf.

40   Ronald Lewis, *Transforming the Appalachian Countryside: Railroads, Deforestation, and Social Change in West Virginia, 1880–1920* (Chapel Hill: University of North Carolina Press, 1998).

41   Catriona Mortimer-Sandilands and Bruce Erickson, *Queer Ecologies: Sex, Nature, Politics, Desire* (Bloomington: Indiana University Press, 2010).

42   Ibid.; for a discussion of the relationship between Queer Studies and Appalachian Studies, see stef m. schuster, "Quaring the Queer in Appalachia," *Appalachian Journal* 46, no. 1–2 (2018): 72–84.

43   Anna Lowenhaupt Tsing, *The Mushroom at the End of the World* (Princeton, NJ: Princeton University Press, 2015), 22–23.

44   McDaniel, "Queer, Rural, Disabled," 153.

45   Sins Invalid, *Skin, Tooth, and Bone: The Basis of the Movement is Our People*, 2nd ed. (San Francisco: Dancers Group, 2019 [2016]).

46   Simi Linton, *Claiming Disability: Knowledge and Identity* (New York: New York University Press, 1998).

47   Ibid., 5.

ABOUT THE AUTHOR

Rebecca-Eli Long is a scholar-activist-artist who uses disability justice principles and lived experiences of disability to imagine a socially just and sustainable future for all bodyminds. Rebecca-Eli's research explores the links between disability, violence, and activism throughout diverse disciplines and geographies. They are especially interested in creative research methodologies that unsettle ableism. Rebecca-Eli is currently a doctoral student in anthropology and gerontology at Purdue University. They hold an MA in Appalachian Studies and a graduate certificate in Aging, Health, and Society from Appalachian State University, where they wrote their thesis on disability and social movements in Appalachia. They can be found online at wwww.rebecca-eli.com.

Performing the Queer Corpo-Rural in Plant Time

Kendall Loyer

Caring for animals, growing plants, analyzing weather patterns in order to plant and harvest crops, cooking, and caring for humans and community are all practices I learned from my ancestors. The practice of acknowledging ancestral ways isn't only something my family does but is a practice in many communities. It is important to make clear that while my family holds this land to be home, we must acknowledge that this land was stolen from its native caretakers long before state lines were construed. While I do not claim indigenous or native identity, and the intricate and necessary conversation that native presence in Appalachia deserves is not within the scope of this brief exploration of time and neoliberalism, I acknowledge the native caretakers of the lands my ancestors call home and discuss it directly in forthcoming work.[1]

My name is Kendall Colleen Loyer. I'm the daughter of Brad and Susan, sister to Nathan, granddaughter of Harold and Vida, Lowell and Ruth Eleanor. I am mother to Tortoise, Luna Tuna, and Juniper MooMoo and wife to Ashley. I am a multigenerational organic farmer who primarily resides in rural Ohio but currently resides in the desert of Southern California, where I sit writing this chapter as an artist, dancer, dancemaker, and budding scholar, learning and unlearning the ways of academia and life.

My maternal ancestors are German immigrants who settled in the mountain community of what is now called Centralia, West Virginia. My paternal ancestors immigrated from Morocco and Lebanon through Spain and Germany and settled in a small farming community in rural Ohio. My dad jokes that my great-grandmother would be amused with the fairness of my skin and the lightness of my hair (I look like a white passing version of Ruth Eleanor). But if you're looking for my "hill cred," it is in my ancestral knowledge and lifeways, not necessarily observed through my geographical location.[2]

The practice I want to discuss in this chapter is one that my family has participated in for as long as there is a record: seed-saving. As a child, I remember opening seed packets scribbled with words and phrases I didn't even understand, but I knew what they were. Most of those packets and seeds were older than I could even conceptualize. "Seeds are alive!" Leah Penniman of Soul Fire Farm reminds us. "They are embryos encased in a protective shell of nourishment. Seeds have evolved resiliency and maintain their vitality for several years, even in harsh conditions."[3] Seed-saving has become a trendy practice since the #growyourown movement came to commodify rural culture into something cute and marketable to the general population of land-owning consumers.[4] However, as Penniman continues to articulate—and I can agree—for many families it was, and still is, an ancestral practice of survival and identity.

Writer Jessica Cory reminds us that "[r]ecounting an experience is another common way for writers to engage with nature and help readers connect to a particular place."[5] Being true to my roots and acknowledging the rural praxis already in place, I know it is necessary to discuss not only labor practices but also to read these practices as a performance of rural resistance.[6] It is also essential that I recount the radical lessons the land, nature, and the place I call home have taught me. As a Dance Studies scholar, I aim to show how this lens can offer a new perspective. Rural spaces provide multiple angles from which to dissect the effects of labor and neoliberal capitalist critiques, but seed-saving quickly presented itself to me as an important practice for building this analysis. It is also a practice of which I have personal and familial knowledge and is an embodied practice about which I am deeply passionate.

It is my assertion that what I call "plant time" in rural communities ruptures the flow of convention and resists the call for militant adherence to linear time.[7] Through the understanding of plant time, I suggest that ancestral knowledges and rural lifeways disrupt this flow. They offer an alternative to linear time and a way to push back against the suffocating oppression of neoliberal capitalism by illuminating the performance of labor, respecting the praxis, and empowering rural communities. They provide a shift and a pushback against the bourgeois and their gluttonous consumption of excess at the cost of our knowledges, happiness, livelihood, and well-being. Dance artist Emily Johnson states, "I view our bodies as everything: culture, history, present, future at once. I'm trying to make a world where performance is a vital part of life, where it's an integral connection to each other-our environment, our stories, our past, present, and future."[8] Here Johnson articulates her ancestral knowledge to reference what I am referring to as plant time. This is the praxis of rural spaces. This is performed resistance.

Microcosm is my friend, my collaborator, my therapist, my performance partner in the rural practice of gardening.[9] We are a communicative duet. Sometimes I tell stories, sing songs my momma taught me, and vent about my day. My dog takes naps in their cool brown soil, and sometimes after a long day of working in their growing rows, I do too. They hold my body from below, and the vines protect me from above. They mostly just listen and hold space for me. Microcosm is my "yarden" (yard garden). While the space they occupy right outside my bedroom window isn't large, the products of their labor are recognized by many. I cultivate their soil to produce chard, kale, radishes, cucumbers, zucchinis, peas, garlic, onions, lettuces, corn, beets, melons, potatoes, beans (fresh and dried), herbs, edible flowers, and, of course, tomatoes. Microcosm is a project my Poopa and I started when I first moved back home to Ohio.[10] Together, we improvise in their chaos. We maneuver up, down, and every way between the unruly vines of the tomatoes and choose which delicate leaves of lettuce to pick. We work piles of dirt into heaps to "hill-up" the potatoes and crawl on our hands and knees to pick beans on plants that have grown so optimally that they have overtaken the preplanned rows and cannot be walked through but can only be crawled under through the tunnels we carefully create as we move the limbs of the plants as we harvest. Microcosm is generous, kind, and a little unruly. My favorite kind of performer and collaborator.

Every year, Microcosm, "goes off," as my momma always says. The production from the plants shifts into the territory of excess due to optimal growing conditions. It is for gifting to my friends, neighbors, the mail carrier, and the local women's shelters. We set up buckets in our yard and at the in-town post office, full of tomatoes and usually cucumbers and zucchinis with signs that say, "free food gifts." This excess harvest is shared with the community, not sold for profit or monetary exchange. This is, on my part, a very careful gesture of mutual aid and care. It is a gift. It is political. It is my performance of resistance to the ideology of neoliberalism.

Scholar Meg Luxton articulates on the structures and expectations of neoliberalism in her 2014 article "Doing Neoliberalism: Perverse Individualism in Personal Life" that "neoliberalism rests on the widespread acceptance that individuals and their households must absorb more of the work necessary to ensure the livelihood and well-being of their members."[11] What Luxton leaves out of her analysis is the recipient of the benefits of the exchanges and the autonomy of gifting. What she states may be a construct of neoliberal ideology from her viewpoint, but it is also a foundational pillar of the system of mutual aid and care.[12] In rural spaces, these ideologies are more supported and effective than those that benefit from the excess of the bourgeois. This can be seen in the exchange of goods or in the sharing of skills and trades.[13]

The Seed and the Tomato: A Classic Metaphor

Out of pure curiosity, I did a quick Google search on how to grow tomatoes from seed.[14] What you see below is the result of said search that appeared repeatedly on different websites.

Step One—Find some trays or pots.
Step Two—Fill the seed container with seed compost.
Step Three—Moisten the surface of the compost.
Step Four—Sprinkle the seeds evenly over the compost.
Step Five—Cover the seed tray.
Step Six—Place the seed tray in a warm place.
Step Seven—Uncover the seedlings once they germinate.

Growing a tomato from a seed sounds simple! Put the seed in the mix of dirt, and you'll grow the food. The process of growing a tomato from a tiny seed is a metaphor for revealing rural labor performance and knowledge. It challenges the idea that the seven-step system listed above isn't quite so simple. It makes visible the performance of the laboring body (in this case, my own) through the quotidian task of growing food for my family and my community. This illuminates the subtleties of rural lifeways and ways of understanding the world through my own growing practice and in collaboration with Microcosm. Microcosm is a metaphor in which to explore alternative rural economies that operate against the paradigm of neoliberal capitalism as well as operating through, around, and directly with said system.

Finding a chore a five-year-old could do was fun for Momma and Poopa. My brother and I alternate between collecting chicken eggs and checking to see if the tomatoes are ready to harvest. Occasionally Poopa picks the green ones to fry up (fried green tomatoes, y'all), but my favorites are the big, fat, bright red ones. I watch Poopa carefully remove the fruit from the plant and gently place it in my tiny hand. I'm supposed to put it in the garden basket, but more often than not, I just take a big bite out of it right there sitting in the dirt surrounded by tomato vines... the way it tastes, how the skin tears and gives way to the juice that inevitably splatters all over my freckled cheeks. I attempt to hide the fact that I took bites out of all the fruits, but the remnants on my face gives me away every time. Poopa and I go up and down row after row of tomato vines searching and analyzing which ones are ready to pick and which ones needed, as he always says, a day or two more of sunshine. We will go out the next afternoon and pick another whole basket full of fruit. Indeed, another day of sunshine. It feels like the most surreal place in the world to me. It feels like magic; that I can just close my eyes for a little bit, and when I open them, the tomato is completely different. I understand there is a certain level of chance one takes and a certain understanding of giving one's plant friends time to produce the most ideal gift for you.

A child's understanding of time is something magical. As an adult, I don't necessarily think that the tomato was waiting to chat with the moon about moving on to other worlds, but maybe the tomatoes flesh just needed a few more hours of sunlight. Maybe the soil finally got a drink of moisture and pushed that last bit of nutrients up through the roots of the plant and out the stems and into the body of the fruit, making it feel and look like perfection, but, then again, perhaps it was a moon chat. In organic gardening, we wait for the fruit to tell us when to pick it, we don't spray it with chemicals to speed up the process, and we don't use seeds that work on a predetermined time schedule. How queer this understanding of time is. How queer the patience. The waiting—the understanding that in this space we wait until the plant is ready to gift us food. This world does not operate for our efficient systems of exchange. It operates within its own temporal understandings. We must wait. We must linger in what I dream is a queer temporality, the land of plant time.

Microcosm looked like a swatch of muddy ground sometimes covered in snow, sometimes with standing puddles of water. This is the phase of rest. Usually nothing was planted for winter cover, but Poopa collected the leaves from the yard and relocated them to this muddy area before the temperatures dropped. The beautifully colored leaves from our giant Oak tree acted as a patchwork quilt for the earth. When it was finally time for the first till of the season, the now decomposing leaves were mixed with the resting soil underneath. The tomato cages got relocated to the edges of the growing space in an attempt to keep my sweet rescue dog Tortoise out of the garden. He loved to dig in the mud, and the winter months provided him with a temptation he simply could not resist. We spread straw on top of the soil once we had cleared a certain crop and wouldn't be planting something else in its place. That also got tilled in with the leaves and the resting soil. During the spring and summer, Microcosm is a completely different place. Some plants have been resting inside and are waiting to be nestled into the ground as soon as the temperature is more agreeable. Others came from a seed that gets placed directly into the ground. It takes a keen eye to understand how much time seedlings can spend outside. They can't get too hot or too cold. They can't get too much sun. They also can't get too much water/rain, and they have to be watched for too much wind exposure. This hardening-off process can take up to a couple weeks.

Growing Plant Time

Microcosm articulates two types of time, linear and plant. Late scholar José Muñoz suggested "straight time" (which I refer to as linear time) as a strong force we must adhere to in order to keep time with the producing world. It is a fast and driving force of obedience for the contemporary capitalist worker. Straight time, in turn, produces surplus value through efficiency that is then commodified by capitalist bourgeois society for extreme profit, almost always at the cost of the livelihood and with no regard to or for the laboring body. In the paradigm of straight time, the body of the laborer is an essential part of the mechanization of production. Small batch growers live and labor in a very queer world. Inhabitants of queer worlds have always been foundational caretakers of nonhuman persons and regarded with great respect within rural communities in spite of "backward" representations outside of these rural spaces. The idea of plant time is an alternative lens through which to view queer corpo-rurality. Queer and straight time through a Muñozian definition and the previously mentioned metaphor of growing a tomato from seed directly engages the notion of queer time as a critique of straight time and, as Muñoz might argue, a gesture toward queer (I'll add rural) futurity. This unconventional understanding of time is what makes rural spaces inherently very queer spaces: the spaces where we are patient and where we wait. The spaces where we linger in plant time.

According to Muñoz, "surplus value," in Marxist terms and as the signature product of straight time, can be explained as the value of work done or volume of commodities produced that exceeds what a worker will need. Within the paradigm of straight time, the goal is to be so efficient that the process of production is essentially the production of surplus value. Within capitalism, surplus value becomes profit in the form of capital value for the capitalist and at the expense of the body and well-being of the worker.

Muñoz asks, what happens when a laboring body deviates from linear time and into plant time? This provocation is described not as an alternative to straight time but as a failure to manage and adhere to its structures. It is a disruption to the flow of surplus capital and its consumption in a globalist, neoliberal-capitalist economy. Queer time doesn't adhere to conventional structures of time. It's out of sync. It's sloppy. It's undisciplined.

Muñoz uses the body of dancer Fred Herko to illustrate this articulation of queer temporality. He shares interviews of artists that collaborated with Herko, stating that he was always late, unkempt, inefficient, undisciplined. He was a drug addict and lacked any markings of professionalism as a dancing and laboring body, from a discussion about his curriculum vitae to stories about him keeping his audience waiting because he was late for his own performances. Muñoz speaks of Herko with loving care and generously gestures toward his "incandescent illumination" (excess not produced for consumption) as a way of living outside the conventions of linear time, not as being as what we would call "a hot mess" in colloquial terms or Momma would refer to as "going off."[15] This was the way Herko lived his life outside of the need to produce the militant fidelity to timeliness and societal pressures to produce work in a certain way.

I pause here to suggest a substitution of bodies and differing labor within the same Muñozian analytical framework of temporality. First, let us assume (because Muñoz asks that we do) that linear time will always be linear time—the norm, the benchmark, the neoliberal "goal" for societal efficiency, as not to disrupt the flows of bourgeois profit. Let us use the same framework for reading queer time, or what Microcosm taught us to understand as plant time, through my performing body in the space of the garden. There are absolutely no hard-and-fast rules about plant time. It might take a few hours of sunshine, and it might take weeks of plants receiving the exact amount of rain, with the exact amount of sunshine, combined with the exact right temperature and cloud cover for these plants to gift us tomatoes. Sometimes the fruit never ripens. Sometimes the sun burns the fruit. Sometimes the flesh of the fruit ruptures, rendering it inedible. Sometimes the friendly neighborhood racoons eat the tomatoes before we can even get to them. One must get comfortable with not being able to predict or foresee the outcomes; it demands the willingness to live with instability and unpredictability.

> Let's start with direct sow additions to the garden. Step one: starting with the spring crops, those that grow in cooler temperatures or bulbs are planted in the fall and grow as soon as it becomes warm enough for harvesting in the spring: radishes, kale, spinach, chard, and peas mostly. Microcosm's crops get rotated to a new location in the 25X50 foot space every year. Once the location is decided, there is a very specific way of planting. Poopa uses a repurposed kite string to mark off straight rows in the garden. We have used this tool for as long as I can remember. It's a two-person job but can be done solo, as the side unattached to the spool has a wooden stake attached to it. Imagine... one side staked into the ground and all you do is release the spool as you walk back down the row, letting the string out as you go. You simply secure the spool on the other side of the rowhead and make sure it's straight enough for your liking. Poopa, a trained carpenter and woodworker, prefers a certain exactitude in this work.
>
> Step two: make a very shallow row in the soil, usually with your finger. Start on one end of the row, following the kite string, gently move away the soil with your finger, just like you are gently petting the head of a tiny kitten. This slight divet in the ground should only

be about an inch or so deep. You get cool farmer bonus points if you get dirt under your nails. It helps if you straddle the row you are making. This begins to mark the space where the walking paths will be. Your knees will squish down the soil enough to indicate this. You follow this process all the way down the row. Then you must add the seeds to the earth. You must know how far away the seeds need to be planted from each other, within the row and across rows. Usually an inch or two is ideal unless planting things like cucumbers, squash, gourds, and pumpkins. You place one tiny seed every one or two inches down the row, sometimes you have multiple rows. Seeds vary in size and shape. Some are round and easy to grab with your fingers, others are flat and require a fingernail or tweezers to catch them. After you place all the seeds in the row, you again start at either end of the row and brush the soil you just displaced back over top of the seeds. As you brush it back over the seeds, gently pat down the soil to cover and secure a safe place for growth.

Final step: give a gentle sprinkle of water, just enough to dampen the soil. Poopa insists on marking the ends of rows with whirling metallic pinwheels. He says it keeps the birds and bunnies away. I think he just likes the sparkle from the sunbeams.

Then you move on to the next row.

As the keeper, the caretaker of these seeds and plants, the guardian of this rural queer space, I keep the food that we need to "put up" for the upcoming winter. Sometimes it will serve as a quick salad or sandwich before I head back to work in the garden, sometimes I eat them fresh, right off the vine—sometimes sitting in the dirt, under the sun, surrounded by tomato vines, just like when I was a tiny human. I ask you to conceptualize this laboring body as a body performing the queer corpo-rural. In his 2011 text *The Darker Side of Modernity: Global Futures, Decolonial Options* semiotician Walter Mignolo suggests, "It is from the body, not the mind that questions arise, and answers are explored."[16] The process of training a body for dancing is no different than training a body to care for and nurture seed beings. There are proper techniques, ways of moving, finding flow, understanding musicality, and interpreting the social and political. These techniques can be learning proper soil constitution and how to make one's own compost for growing seeds or how deep to plant the seeds in order to stimulate germination. How much water do they really need? What is the proper temperature at which to keep the germinating seeds? Which seeds are viable to plant and which aren't? How do I pick which seeds to keep and from which tomato? Which pots, trays, or other vessels are optimal for starting seeds? When do I start the seeds? When do I take them outside, and how do I introduce them to the outside elements? What happens when those things you learned don't work optimally? How do you troubleshoot? How do you know when to let go of what you know and try something else? You will quickly learn that nothing happens on time, nothing goes as planned, and time is rendered irrelevant.

In the paradigm of linear time, machines produce with militant precision. High volumes of sameness, aesthetic replicas, an endless supply of perfect specimens that can be created at the flip of a switch. Food is delivered to your doorstep. It is severed from its origin, detached from the labor of its growing process. Sometimes it's grown in a lab with the DNA of bacteria creating what is known as a genetically modified organism (GMO). It is grown in fields covered in chemicals to keep the bugs from damaging the aesthetic presentation of the product.

In the world of plant time, plants produce when they are cared for properly. Gardeners spend time with their plants, sleeping alongside their dogs, protected by their vines. They touch them and even sing to them. The plants produce on their own time schedule and grow when they want to. It might take months; it might take weeks. The gardener communicates with nonhuman life forms, nonhuman persons, not machines. When the plant is done producing it stops, and the gardener offers the body of the plant to the compost, where it is turned into soil for planting the next round of seeds the following season. The earth supports and is supported in this process. Nothing is the same. Each tomato looks different than the others. Sometimes tomatoes are perfectly spherical, sometimes they are lumpy or bulbous. They grow in all different colors. Sometimes there are bug bites, and there are always weeds to pull. An organic garden is sometimes every bit of the "hot mess" I mentioned earlier. Perhaps it just incandescently illuminates.

Invisibility, Hypervisibility, and Performed Resistance

Recently, in a conversation with my dear colleagues and friends, dance-makers Josie Bettman and Olana Flynn, I was talking about things in rural spaces that aren't seen—transactions and exchanges that are secret, on purpose.[17] They were concerned that the invisibility may lessen the impact of the exchanges. This conversation sent my mind spiraling into thought of what might be gained and lost in this secretive praxis. It excites me to think about the idea of work, labor, and transaction as an embodied praxis that happens on the periphery, in the unmonitored margins.

Whether our eyes see the work, the labor, the performance, the exchange, they happen. These things have value and real-life consequences that get played out on living breathing human bodies. Rural bodies are left out of the conversation within academia most of the time, unless, of course, to reference the decay and downward spiral of the working class or of the capitalist benefits of rural spaces. Remaining steadfast to one's personal, familial, and community needs under the guise of invisibility allows for more autonomous care and community-oriented activity. However, it also allows for more exploitation of the already vulnerable.

When I created Microcosm, I was met with joy from my immediate neighbors. They were excited that they would get fresh organic tomatoes, and they did. I was met with rules and regulations by local political figures. I was interrogated about where I purchased my seed and soil and questioned about the aesthetics of my garden, how manicured it would be, and how I would make sure that it wouldn't attract excess bugs. You see, I come from the land of big commercial farms that are brand-allegiant to only Monsanto products. Microcosm and my family's praxis of seed-saving caused quite a stir. It made visible alternative lifeways and disrupted and challenged the norms of Monsanto's rhetoric.

My yarden quickly became the local figurehead of anti-neoliberal resistance. It also became hypervisible to those who disagreed with my alternative ways and made working outside potentially dangerous. Some local folks would sometimes drive by slowly in an attempt to try to intimidate me by screaming sexist, homophobic, and degrading things (which won't be repeated here) at me while I worked. When they saw me out and about in town, some even attempted to drive me off the road or would drive threateningly close behind me. They would stare at me confrontationally in the store.

The situation escalated when someone, under the cover of darkness, vandalized our property by dumping acid on my plants. It turned my cucumbers, tomatoes, lettuces, and herbs to chemically burnt dust.

Months of labor destroyed with a hateful toss of a bucket of unknown acid. The once beautiful rich green leaves crumbled in the breeze. They were literal dust. Things certainly quieted down after that, but for me the work continued. The contaminated soil was collected and removed—fresh compost and natural soil boosters were added in its place. The old soil is being rehabilitated over time through exposure to the earth's natural elements and addition of natural soil boosters in our colloquially referred to "rehab center."[18]

In the end, the hostility only proved to me that the act of rural resistance meant putting my body on the line (through my labor) to advocate for what I feel to be an important intervention in the world. It showed me that sometimes the secrets, the exchanges on the periphery and in the margins, can do more work than those that become visible, like Microcosm. But on the other hand, I'm honored and proud to say that my continued environmental work in my community has found me teaching local organic gardening classes and conversing with local farmers about how to convert their land to more sustainable farming practices. It is in these moments that together we work against the conventional notions of linear time. We critique the adherence to neoliberal principles of production and seize the means for our collective selves. It is in these moments of relying on ancestral practices that we find the greatest resistance to the entities that are created to keep us consistently at odds with each other.

I remind you that when we trace and acknowledge the labor of caring for a seed through its germination, becoming a seedling, being planted in the ground, all the way to its arrival into the world as food, and then into the hands of our community, we acknowledge the power of hidden labor. We honor the performance of resistance in rural spaces, and we replace neoliberal ideology with mutual aid and care for each other and the nonhuman entities in our care. In the casual words of my Cornbread Communist comrades, this is how we eat the rich, like a goddamn mater sandwich.[19]

NOTES

1   My forthcoming, currently untitled dissertation, University of California, Riverside, 2022.

2   For one explanation of "hill cred," listen to Drew and Meg Hubbard, "Episode 27: Hill Cred," *Speaking Over the Mountains* (podcast), August 8, 2018, accessed October 7, 2021, https://www.listennotes.com/podcasts/speaking-over-the/episode-27-hill-cred-QguyrRzD_qZ.

3   Leah Penniman, *Farming While Black: Soul Fire Farm's Practical Guide to Liberation on the Land* (Hartford, VT: Chelsea Green Publishing, 2018), 158.

4   #growyourown became a popular hashtag on social media platforms when land-owning folx began converting yards to gardens and growing specially marketed heirloom and organic seeds. In plain language, rural practices became commodified and trendy. They reduced a lifeway to a simplistic hashtag and "fun" activist project.

5   Jessica Cory, ed., *Mountain Piled Upon Mountains: Appalachian Nature Writing in the Anthropocene* (Morgantown: West Virginia University Press, 2019), 5.

6   Rural praxis is what I call the lifeways of rural communities.

7   "Plant time" is an operational paradigm that queers human understandings of time by focusing on embodied articulations of plants. Plant time is a resistive practice that disrupts settler-colonial time and, therefore, shifts the movements and growth of these nonhuman persons as political.

8   Emily Johnson, "Choreographers Statements," *Dance Research Journal* 48, no. 1 (April 2016): 36.

9   I will utilize this proposed duet between my partner Microcosm and myself to analyze the concepts of time and the anti-neoliberal praxis of rural lifeways.

10   Poopa's legal name is Bradley Eugene Loyer. He is my father. March 6, 1949–July 13, 2019. He (and Microcosm) taught me everything I know about gardening, growing, and saving seeds. This is an acknowledgment of his labor and his love.

11   Meg Luxton, "Doing Neoliberalism: Perverse Individualism in Personal Life," in *Neoliberalism and Everyday Life*, ed. Susan Braedley and Meg Luxton (Montreal: McGilll-Queens University Press, 2014), 163.

12   I conceptualize mutual aid as a voluntary reciprocal exchange of resources and services for mutual benefit. Please see the extensive mutual aid work of the organization Queer Appalachia, queerappalachia.com.

13   Growing up I thought this exchange practice was the norm. For example, maybe a neighbor's cucumbers didn't do well, so we would exchange our vibrant cucumbers for something we didn't have or also didn't do well. This can be said for milk, eggs, meat, and any kind of fruit, vegetable, or flower. This can also be observed in skills trade. For example, my father was a plumber and woodworker. He would fix plumbing or build things in exchange for work in an area he wasn't skilled in or needed help with.

14   My family is known by our community for growing delicious tomatoes. Growing tomatoes is part of my ancestral knowledge passed down to me from my Poopa.

15   "Going off" is what my momma says when she notices the garden is growing and producing faster than we can consume its gifts.

16   Walter Mignolo, *The Darker Side of Modernity: Global Futures, Decolonial Options* (Durham, NC: Duke University Press. 2011), xxiv.

17   More information about these artists can be found at josiebettman.com and Olanaflynn.com.

18   The rehab center is a separate space in our garden where certain plants are given extra love and care in order to nurse them back to optimal health.

19   The phrase is taken from the organization's Instagram account, but you can enjoy a pdf version of the collaboratively produced "Cornbread Communist Manifesto," 2019, accessed October 12, 2021, https://tinyurl.com/k498kdst.

ABOUT THE AUTHOR

Kendall Loyer is a PhD candidate in Critical Dance Studies at the University of California, Riverside. She holds a BA in Dance Performance from Columbia College Chicago and a MFA in Experimental Choreography from the University of California, Riverside. Loyer is a dancer, dancemaker, dramaturge, educator, photographer, and creative writer. Her movement practice investigates memory, embodied processes of remembering, and themes of loss and displacement. Her doctoral research investigates queer rurality within folk practices and performance within the region of Appalachia. She investigates the radical possibilities of folk lifeways to reimagine a community analytic that actively works against the necropolitical violence of racial capitalism.

Tree Sit Blockades and Queer Liberation

Chessie Oak

As I write this, I am suspended more than fifty feet in the air on a platform in a chestnut oak tree that stands in the path of environmental destruction. I live in one of the tree sits in the Yellow Finch blockade, now a collection of three tree sits located on the proposed path of the Mountain Valley Pipeline and a nearby camp on the ground that directly supports the tree sits. We have been preventing deforestation and construction of the Mountain Valley Pipeline for more than a year and a half on this stretch of land by living high up in these trees, putting our lives on the line should they try to cut the trees down to build the pipeline.[1] The Mountain Valley Pipeline is a forty-two-inch diameter, 303-mile-long pipeline that will carry fracked gas from the Marcellus and Utica shale region in northern West Virginia to Southern Virginia for export. If completed, it will cross 1,108 bodies of water, 3 major aquifers, 32 acres of wetlands, and 235 miles of forest, including the Appalachian Trail and the Jefferson National Forest, disturbing the ecosystems of 23 federally listed threatened or endangered species and coming within 50 feet of 118 homes.[2] Pipelines are incredibly dangerous; on average in the so-called United States, a pipeline catches fire every four days and explodes every eleven days, killing someone every twenty-six days, and causing almost $1.3 million in property damage every day.[3]

This tree sit blockade is part of the broader campaign of Appalachians Against Pipelines against the Mountain Valley Pipeline, and it is part of the rich history of resistance against the fossil fuel industry and extraction in Appalachia. People have been resisting the exploitation of these mountains, the corporations carrying out this exploitation, and the governments that allow and support it for centuries. To highlight a few of my favorite examples:

In Tennessee from 1891 to 1893, former coal miners whose labor had been replaced by unpaid prisoners rebelled, starting what was called the Coal Creek War and resulting in the repeal of the convict lease system in Tennessee.[4] In 1921, at the Battle of Blair Mountain, thousands of coal miners went on strike as part of a series of armed insurrections against coal corporations in West Virginia.[5] In 1965, sixty-one-year-old Ollie Combs and her two sons sat in front of a bulldozer to stop strip mining on her farm in Kentucky.[6] Despite decades of bribery and coercion, Larry Gibson and the Stanley family refused to sell their land to coal companies, and to this day their land remains unexploited.[7]

Grassroots campaigns like the Coal River Mountain Valley Watch and Radical Action for Mountain Peoples' Survival have organized against mountaintop removal mining for years. More recently, as fracking industries have come to Appalachia, organizations have risen up in resistance, including Appalachia Resist! and communities organizing in the Ohio River Valley against the proposed ethane cracker plants and petrochemical hub that would make plastics out of fracked gas. Since 2014, people in the area have also been resisting fracking by organizing against the Mountain Valley Pipeline, fighting through the courts, regulatory processes, and on the ground through direct action in affected communities. Appalachians Against Pipelines is a loose organization that was "formed" in 2018 and includes people from affected communities, activists that have been fighting extractive industry for years—especially mountaintop removal mining and other pipelines—and young people, especially current and former college students. Appalachians Against Pipelines uses nonviolent direct action to impede construction of the Mountain Valley Pipeline in West Virginia and Virginia, primarily using the tactics of aerial blockades, such as tree sits and monopods, as well as lockdowns (locking oneself to a piece of machinery or something similar so that work cannot be done on that construction site).[8] A pair of tree sits along with a monopod and skypod were used on the top of Peters Mountain to halt drilling under the Appalachian Trail long enough for the Mountain Valley Pipeline to lose vital permits.[9] A local school teacher locked down to her old Ford Pinto in the path of the pipeline where she lives in West Virginia.[10] Altogether, the actions of Appalachians Against Pipelines have prevented construction for hundreds of days and cost the

Mountain Valley Pipeline, by their estimation, hundreds of thousands of dollars in delays and move-around costs.

To blockade is to occupy space in a way that disrupts the day-to-day exploitation and oppression committed by the capitalist, colonial hetero-patriarchy that we live under. Capitalist, colonial heteropatriarchy is a system of power relations maintained through violence in which trade, industry, land, and, formerly, people are controlled by private owners for profit. Political control is grounded in the occupation of land by settlers, the exploitation of the land and its peoples, and in a ruling class of rich, settler, heterosexual, cisgender men. The Yellow Finch tree sit blockade/ground support camp disrupts the system not only by stopping pipeline destruction but also by being a community in which the vast majority of us are queer/trans and are doing what we can to upend settler colonial-ism and contribute to active decolonization of peoples and land. Part of why I love living at this blockade is that my queerness and my identity as nonbinary don't make me an outcast; they are part of a collective identity. The capitalist system thrives by isolating people from each other, creating and enforcing hierarchies and divisions between us, and maintaining a sense of loneliness and powerlessness. By living collectively in queer community, we disrupt these attempts to centralize power into the hands of the privileged few. This sense of community and disruption of power centralization extends beyond just the people who live at this blockade; this blockade would likely not continue to exist without the financial and physical support of local people, queer and straight, and organizations like Queer Appalachia who visit us, bringing us supplies and boosting morale.

Living in the midst of nature for a while, I have observed that the natural world is not structured around hierarchies and binaries. It is rather a network of interrelationships between organisms and species that enable the survival of them all. Trees provide homes for birds and small animals; fungi and micro-organisms help bring nutrients out of the soil for plants; animal waste and decaying organisms provide food for worms, bugs, and more; woodpeckers eat pests out of trees; bees and other pollinators ensure plant species' survival and reproduction. In many ways, life at this blockade mimics this web of interrelationships; much of the day-to-day work here is centered around community survival and taking care of each other. Everyone autonomously does the tasks they enjoy doing or feel like doing that day—chopping wood, cooking meals, security shifts, organizing our library, stocking our food pantry, building structures, carrying water and donations up the hill, etc.—and collectively we survive. This way of relating to each other and surviving flies in the face of binaries and hierarchies, of managers and power and oppression. Society is constructed in such a way that binaries of inferiority/superiority seem natural and inevitable—woman/man, nature/civilization, body/mind, emotion/logic and strategy—with the "inferiors" linked together and the "superiors" linked together. This blockade refuses to exist within these binaries, complicating both the categories and their relationships to each other. For example, are we nature defending itself or an offshoot of civilization? In these ways, this collective of queer activists disrupts hierarchies created by capitalist, colonial heteropatriarchy.

Talking with some of the other people who live here around the campfire, one of our favorite aspects of living in the woods in a queer community is the lack of screens, mirrors, and the hetero-male gaze (the way in which women and people perceived as women are depicted and interpreted as sexual objects for the pleasure of the male viewer). Here, our bodies are for the physical labor of survival and care work, for keeping ourselves and our friends nourished, for climbing, building, making art, singing, playing, dancing—not for society to ostracize, ridicule, or judge. There is no need to perform gender or to "prove" our genders and/or queerness to others; we aren't being tested all the time; our pronouns will be used, our identities respected, and our genders/queerness are not the most central part of how people perceive us. Gender is culturally created, and in our own queer subculture, we have room to create our own gender relations, while disrupting and deconstructing those of society.

Painted on the underside of one of the tree sit platforms are the words "stop men." I have seen many of the cismen who visit the blockade, including local supporters, stare up at it, bewildered by the blatant challenging of gendered societal power dynamics. While the message behind these words is mostly metaphorical, i.e., "stop patriarchy" or "stop men from behaving in ways that uphold the roles and power dynamics that society conditions into us," it also takes on a more literal and specific message by being on the bottom of the tree sit. The majority of the human foes of this blockade are men—the police and pipeline workers who have to read the words "stop men" as they photograph us, arrest people on the ground, and eventually extract or starve out the tree sits, and the corporate executives and corrupt government officials who the police and pipeline workers serve. Those who violently uphold capitalist, colonial heteropatriarchy and those who profit most from its exploitation of land and life are overwhelmingly white men.

However, it is important to acknowledge that even those who vehemently oppose colonization, capitalism, and heteropatriarchy are often still complicit in them, and we must be critical of ourselves. Resisting the system does not make us immune to its benefits to people with certain identities at the expense of others, nor does it make us exempt from its history and legacy and the need for reparations to and reconciliation with those that historically and presently experience systemic violences. Furthermore, living in resistance does not mean we are incapable of committing and perpetuating the same kinds of violences that the system does, even and especially unintentionally, and we must take responsibility and accountability for this. As a predominantly white camp, the fact that we are even living at this blockade is the result of genocidal colonial violence by many of our ancestors against the Cherokee, Monacan, Tutelo-Saponi, and other Indigenous peoples of this region. What does it mean to occupy this stolen land as majority white people, while also reclaiming the path of pipeline destruction as a space to build queer community? What privileges do we have—skin color, health/physical ability, US citizenship, familial wealth, etc.—that make us able us to do this work, and how can we work to make it so that people without these privileges are just as able? How can we use our privileges to fight for the elimination of the system of power and oppression that allows only people with certain identities to have and experience privilege? These are questions that we don't have and maybe never will have perfect answers for, which makes it all the more important to keep asking and discussing them. While we challenge the system, we must also challenge ourselves.

To blockade is also to imagine a better world. For me, a sustainable future is a world in which housing, food, clean air and water, mental and physical health care, education, and all other basic needs are met for all people. A world with no prisons, no borders, no police, no corporations, and no hierarchies of power, privilege, exploitation, and oppression. A world organized as communities and tribal kinship groups rather than nuclear families and colonial states. A world in which all people are respected and allowed to live freely, and we have a respectful and reciprocal relationship with nature. All of these are integral parts of queer liberation. This future is possible—all we have to do is create it and keep recreating it and acting it out in our everyday lives and actions. This blockade, and its imagining and enactment of a different world, are certainly far from perfect, and eventually it will get torn down. But even though this blockade is temporary and will eventually be destroyed, it has cost the Mountain Valley Pipeline a few hundred thousand dollars and has not only decreased the feasibility of this pipeline but also changed the calculations for future extractive projects. Once this blockade is gone, we'll get to try again, to rebuild again, to use what we've learned here to reimagine and act toward better worlds again.

NOTES

1   Laurence Hammack, "After a Year in the Trees, Opponents Continue to Block Work on the Pipeline," *Roanoke Times*, September 5, 2019, accessed October 8, 2021, https://tinyurl.com/76ww9mc7. To follow and support the activities of the Yellow Finch Tree Sits, you can find Appalachians Against Pipelines on Facebook and Instagram (@appalachiansagainstpipelines), and on Twitter (@stopthemvp), You can donate to their work directly at https://tinyurl.com/j348mtp5.

2   Federal Energy Regulatory Commission, "Mountain Valley Pipeline and Equitrans Expansion Project: Final Environmental Impact Statement," June 23, 2017, accessed October 8, 2021, https://tinyurl.com/22nem6mx.

3   Matt Kelso, "Pipeline Incidents Continue to Impact Residents," *Fractracker Alliance*, December 7, 2018, accessed October 8, 2021, https://www.fractracker.org/2018/12/pipeline-incidents-impact-residents.

4   Karin Shaprio, *A New South Rebellion: The Battle against Convict Labor in the Tennessee Coal Fields, 1871–1896* (Chapel Hill: University of North Carolina Press, 1998).

5   Robert Shogan, *The Battle of Blair Mountain: The Story of America's Largest Labor Uprising* (Boulder, CO: Westview Press, 2004).

6   Bill Strode, "Widow vs. Bulldozer—Has Mrs. Combs Beaten the Strip Miners?" *Courier-Journal*, November 28, 1965, accessed October 8, 2021, https://tinyurl.com/yhasamxx.

7   Ken Ward Jr., "Remembering the 'Keeper of the Mountains,'" *Coal Tattoo* (blog), *Charleston Gazette-Mail*, September 10, 2012, accesssed October 8, 2021, http://blogs.wvgazettemail.com/coaltattoo/2012/09/10/remembering-the-keeper-of-the-mountains.

8   Earth First!, *Direct Action Manual*, 3rd ed., (Oakland: AK Press, 2015), accessed October 8, 2021, https://issuu.com/earthfirstjournal/docs/dam_3rd_edition.

9   Anonymous, "After the Monopod: Nutty and the Anti-Pipeline Fight in Appalachia," It's Going Down, August 14, 2018, accessed October 8, 2021, https://itsgoingdown.org/after-the-monopod-nutty-anti-pipeline-fight-in-appalachia.

10   GJEP Staff, "West Virginia: Retired School Teacher Blockades Mountain Valley Pipeline," Global Justice Ecology Project, July 31, 2018, accessed October 8, 2021, https://globaljusticeecology.org/west-virginia-retired-schoolteacher-blockades-mountain-valley-pipeline.

ABOUT THE AUTHOR

Chessie Oak is a young, white, queer/nonbinary tree sitter at the Yellow Finch blockade in Elliston, Virginia. They also identify as a full-time anarchist, a nerd, a musician, and a former college student and wage laborer. They would like to emphasize that there is nothing special about them—no achievements or qualifications or anything else of the kind—that led them to where they are now besides their passion. To learn more about, support, or get involved with Appalachians Against Pipelines, see https://www.facebook.com/appalachiansagainstpipelines.

Creating the Queer-Appalachian Archive

Myths and Electricity: The Queer Appalachia Project and Unconventional Queer Archives

Maxwell Cloe

Queerness and the Imagined Appalachia

Appalachia is a region of myths. For decades, Appalachia has existed in the national imagination as an alien wasteland.[1] The mere mention of the mountains conjures images of toothless hillbillies and dusty coal miners tragically fighting for survival in a landscape that is wildly uninhabitable for anyone daring to enter.[2] Appalachia is, for many, an empty spot on the map of the United States where most people seemingly live without electricity, running water, or the modern liberal politics of the metropoles down below.

The conglomeration of blame, myth, fear, and self-righteousness that surrounds the popular discourse on Appalachia applies doubly for the queer people living in the region. Many films, such as John Boorman's 1972 *Deliverance* or Ang Lee's 2005 *Brokeback Mountain*, about queer people in rural areas overwhelmingly depict LGBTQIA+ life in these regions as inherently dire and almost always painful.[3] In his 2005 book *In a Queer Time and Place*, cultural theorist Jack Halberstam uses the term "metronormativity" to describe this culturally dominant understanding that the queer and the rural are incompatible.[4]

Metronormative narratives treat rural regions as a spatial closet out of which LGBTQIA+ people must emerge by moving to the city and realizing "the full expression of the sexual self."[5] If queer people exist in a rural area, they are either in hiding, "out" but only suffering due to a multitude of social and political factors, or simply delusional and inauthentically queer. This assessment, of course, is inaccurate, as it depends on a binary understanding of queer visibility (one is either "in" or "out" of the closet) that simply does not account for the wide range of tactics that rural queer people employ to control their own visibility, safety, and flourishing.[6]

In her 2016 essay, "In Plain(s) Sight," historian Carly Thomsen argues that metronormativity additionally constructs a contradictory sexual and racial conception of rurality. She explains that metronormative thinking necessarily depends on the popular understanding of the rural as entirely white and straight to make these regions easy to condemn from "liberal political commitments" focused purely on superficial demographic breakdown.[7] Metronormative narratives require flattened racial depictions of the rural in order to advocate against it, even if such a flattening erases the presence of racial and sexual communities that metronormative narratives claim to be in the best interests of.

As a result of the sheer magnitude of contemporary liberal theorizing and self-aggrandizement about the region, Appalachia has become the most mythological rural area in the United States and the prime scapegoat for metronormative narratives.[8] It is *the* spatial closet of the nation—abandon all hope queers who enter here. In this chapter, I look at the political and scholarly ramifications of these metronormative narratives, particularly the ways in which they erase any presence of queer-Appalachian people, networks, and cultures from "official" archives of the region. In opposition to this erasure, however, many queer-Appalachians—such as those associated with the Queer Appalachia project and related social media accounts—have archived their experiences through a multitude of unconventional methods, both online and offline. Using contemporary theories of queer archives and oral histories from LGBTQIA+ Appalachians, I analyze how such unconventional archives act as a potentially radical means of not just rural queer archiving but queer archiving regardless of geography.

Appalachia, Archives, Academia, and Absence

Unsurprisingly, the metronormative erasure (or simply ignorance, which nevertheless leads to erasure) of LGBTQIA+ Appalachian lives also plagues academic and archival accounts of the region. This erasure is readily evident in the immense lack of Appalachian LGBTQIA+ texts, artifacts, or other records in state and academic archives. One personal example: during my first week living in Morgantown, West Virginia, I got in contact with the West Virginia and Regional History Center. The center touts "public access to materials that show the history and culture of West Virginia and the Central Appalachian region," spanning "over 3.7 miles of shelf space ... multiple terabytes of digital content."[9] Inquiring about the archive's collection of artifacts and texts relating to LGBTQIA+ Appalachian history, I was met with an email that informed me that the archive could offer me "a single item collection," consisting of a small pamphlet for WVU's Homophile Awareness League. This lack of queer artifacts (or, just as importantly, the failure to categorize already present artifacts as LGBTQIA+ adjacent) is common throughout many academic archives, especially those in locations like Appalachia where queerness has historically faced policing and persecution.

One of the most direct effects of this absence in academic archives is the lack of academic scholarship on queerness in Appalachia, which depends on such archives. Though her 1999 historiography of Appalachian scholarship "Beyond the Mountains: The Paradox of Women's Place in Appalachian History" focuses almost exclusively on straight, cisgender women, Barbara Ellen Smith's conclusions as to why scholarship on the region trends toward the straight male are still particularly relevant to discussions on queer exclusion. She explains that while scholarship in Appalachian Studies has "reclaimed the Appalachian past from condescension and obscurity" by focusing on the region's populist labor movements, it has done so in a way that frames the region's history as "virtually all male."[10] This, according to Smith, establishes an "implicit metanarrative of Appalachian historiography" that is "deeply gendered: 'mountaineers' (and their academic advocates) act to defend the female Appalachia," a construction that not only pushes women into a marginal space but completely erases people that live outside of a heterosexual, cisgender existence.[11] In the decades following Smith's assessment, Appalachian Studies has expanded, including numerous important works discussing not only the radical labor history of the region but the history of women and people of color as well. However, as a 2015 historiography of Appalachian Studies argues, the discipline has done little to incorporate the voices and history of the region's queer population; put bluntly, "recognition of LGBT Appalachians and the integration of queer theory have been even slower to impact Appalachian Studies than theories of gender and race/ethnicity have been."[12]

This is not to suggest, of course, that no academic treatment of LGBTQIA+ communities in Appalachia exists. Recent developments in queer theory and history, such as Mary Gray's 2009 book *Out in the Country* and Colin Johnson's 2013 work *Just Queer Folks*, do not focus on Appalachia specifically but nevertheless provide invaluable insight into queer life in rural spaces, further signaling an increasing academic visibility of rural queerness. A handful of recent long-form writings,[13] as well as a 2020 book on queer storytelling in Appalachia, also suggest that the intersections of LGBTQIA+ and Appalachian identities are becoming increasingly relevant and necessary for understanding the current landscape of queer history and theory.[14]

Theory and Methods

Where academic archives have failed to preserve and document the voices of queer-Appalachians,[15] many queer-Appalachians themselves have worked to construct archives of their own experiences and the experiences of the networks of queer people around them. In addition to archiving their experiences through conventional mediums like photographs and historical documents, these queer-Appalachians employ unconventional methodologies and content in order to include a wider range of experiences.

In my discussion of unconventional queer archives, I rely primarily on the archival theories of Jack Halberstam and critical theorist Ann Cvetkovich. In her 2003 book *An Archive of Feelings*, Cvetkovich argues that decades of queer trauma and exclusion from mainstream society has led to unconventional forms of documentation, "giving rise to new genres of expression ... and new forms of monuments, rituals, and performances" that can be read and used as a means of preserving queer emotions, memories, and history.[16] This "unusual archive," Cvetkovich argues, relies on materials that are "frequently ephemeral" in order to reflect the impermanence of queer trauma, which is often "marked by forgetting and dissociation [and] seems to leave behind no records at all."[17] The ephemerality of queer archival contents thus does not solely refer to the fragility of the archive's physical contents. Rather, it takes into account the queer feelings, memories, and anecdotes that surround and inform these physical objects in ways that conventional and objective approaches to archiving simply cannot.

Following Cvetkovich's understanding of queer archives as rooted in feeling and ephemerality, Jack Halberstam similarly approaches the archive as more than a physical repository of artifacts and "official" narratives. Instead of just a physical place and collection, Halberstam sees archives as a "theory of cultural relevance, a construction of collective memory, and a complex record of queer activity."[18] The creation and maintenance of a queer archive—which Halberstam notes is not just the role of academic archivists but also queer "cultural producers" like artists and musicians—thus becomes an act of political resistance in opposition to the homophobic and transphobic institutions that seek to erase the lives and experiences of queer people.[19] Moreover, Halberstam's abstract definition of archives opens the potential for many objects, processes, or narratives to be objects, even unintentionally.

In an effort to reflect the emotional and subjective dimension of queer archiving, I center my analysis of rural queer archives on oral histories that I conducted with queer-Appalachian archivists and activists; direct quotes from these interviews appear throughout this chapter. I conducted these oral history sessions face-to-face with the narrator, usually in their home or a location that they knew well. I came prepared to each oral history session with a list of questions relating to queer archiving to prompt discussion.[20] I also made an effort to follow the conversation to wherever the narrator took it, understanding that deviations and tangents are an essential facet of the narrator's emotional relationship to their queerness, their rurality, and their approaches to archiving. This concerted effort to restrict myself from directing the conversation emerges from oral history methods laid out by historian Nan Boyd in her 2012 article "Talking about Sex." Boyd explains that one of her principal errors in her early oral history work was her insistence on a questionnaire and fairly rigid adherence to her questions, which "seemed to restrict the narrator's authority" instead of letting the narrator lead the conversation.[21] She felt her tendency to guide the session narrowed the field of discussion, lowering the potential for illuminating deviations in the conversation.

Mobile Archives: The Queer Appalachia Project and Social Media Archives

One contemporary and particularly unconventional archive is the Instagram account for the Queer Appalachia project, an art and politics collective dedicated to reconfiguring public notions of Appalachia to include the experiences of people who are not the straight, white cismen who fill popular depictions of the region. During my oral history session with Mamone, the founder and former director of the Queer Appalachia project,[22] they explained that the Instagram account began in 2015 with a simple request for queer-Appalachians to "send us your Electric Dirt."[23]

Such a declaration catalyzes the potential that digital media—particularly social media—holds for the expansion of the independent queer archives today and into the future. This phrase is, at first glance, an oxymoron. Electric: signifying futurity, wealth, urbanity, machination. Dirt: signifying rusticity, poverty, rurality, manual labor. To combine them highlights the paradoxes that drive metronormative narratives about the incompatibility of rural and queer identities, as well as the incompatibility of Appalachia and the political left. Additionally, this phrase underscores the necessary role that digital technology does and will continue to play in rural queer preservation and organizing.

The "Electric Dirt" that fills the Queer Appalachia Instagram page is, thus, a call to Appalachian people to embrace and dismantle those narratives, while simultaneously urging those who believe those narratives to reconsider their veracity. The result is an ever-expanding, communally generated archive that is less bound by the sexual politics of the federal, state, and local governments than conventional physical archives. To quote Mamone:

> [Before smartphones] you had to have access to higher education, usually a master's degree in archiving, folklore, being some kind of historian. You had to have some kind of something to decide who got to be omitted from their own history and who got to be recorded. One thing we do is we give that the middle finger.[24]

Conventional physical archives are often dependent on the structures of power that academic and governmental institutions uphold. What is preserved and documented (or omitted) is necessarily at the hands of a hierarchy that typically excludes many of the communities that it purports to represent. Instances of erasure like the National Archive's censorship of anti-Trump sentiment in protest signs or the lack of any *academic* queer archives in West Virginia illustrate that the content and work of academic archives is typically beholden to the dominant, and usually conservative, morality of local, state, and federal governments.[25] Additionally, in his analysis of biographies of transgender people, Jack Halberstam notes that the person inserting themselves into another person's life or networks (the biographer in Halberstam's case and the archivist or academic in mine) creates a marginalizing distinction between the researcher and the subject.[26] As such, even the attempt to include marginalized voices by those within the academy is often fraught with an othering mentality that only leads to trivialized, flattened, or otherwise inaccurate depictions of queerness. Furthermore, the process of moving into other spaces to conduct research often faces the (justified) resistance of subjects who are wary of the archivists' potentially elitist intentions, reducing the range of what appears in the archive.[27]

A digital archive that makes use of the decentralized and horizontal structure of the internet (horizontal and decentralized in the sense that anyone can post without having to appeal to a chain of higher-ups) like the Queer Appalachia Instagram page provides a way around many of the hang-ups of conventional archives. Like conventional archives, Mamone acted as a mediator who decided what gets in or what does not based on what they find "real interesting," meaning that a certain level of gatekeeping takes place, as an uninhibited stream of posting would potentially lead to harmful, bigoted, and irrelevant content being posted.[28] Unlike conventional archives, Mamone, the people that they collaborate with, and the new leadership of the Instagram account are queer-Appalachians working to represent queer-Appalachians in a way that is dignified, responsible, and cognizant of the racial and class factors that contribute to the modern LGBTQIA+ Appalachian landscape.[29] As a result, the content that appears in the Queer Appalachia archive comes almost entirely from queer-Appalachian people representing themselves in a manner that they see fit. These posts depict queer-Appalachian people with an understanding that their existence is an intrinsic part of Appalachian life, queer or otherwise.

In his 2016 essay "Digital Oral History and the Limits of Gay Sex," John Howard outlines what he sees as the role that digital media and communication will play in the future of queer research. The advantages that digital media affords to oral historians similarly apply to the process of digital archiving. As Howard notes, the rapidity of online communication enables one of his narrators to exercise "his own agency and power by precisely stating the terms for publishing his interview" in real time, all while maintaining a digital record of the exchange and consent.[30] Similarly, people submitting to the Queer Appalachia Instagram account can navigate ongoing archival consent by including in their submission message the exact terms under which the image is to be posted, captioned, and tagged.[31] Since Instagram allows edits on posts, any request to remove names, alter captions, or delete photos can be quickly honored without the need to deal with any bureaucracy. Howard also explains that the casual nature and familiarity of digital interactions can lead to a bond between narrator and researcher that overcomes anxieties over permissible speech and generates "challenges and possibilities for shattering normative structures of sexual pleasure and desirability."[32]

The erotic, explicit, and diverse images that appear on Queer Appalachia's Instagram account illustrate that the relationship between the digital archive and the submitter is likewise less limited by the hesitation or censorship that often characterize institutional archives. As Jon Coleman, director of the Faulkner-Morgan Archives in Kentucky, explains, queer content in institutional archives often experiences rejection or erasure stemming from conservative ideas about queer visibility, representation, and public notions of respectability:

> "Would they want it all? What about the super erotic stuff? What happens if that culture changes? What if a state senator really gets a bee in his bonnet about it and makes a big deal?"[33]

Many of the "Electric Dirt" posts, then, demonstrate that the internet, particularly social media, allows for a broader tolerance of queer content, both sexually explicit and otherwise. For example, the December 31, 2019, post (figure 1) shows two naked people—one nonbinary person and one woman—embracing and kissing underwater. Along with the ample amount of bare skin that might raise the suspicions of the conservative senator that Coleman mentions, the post's caption states, "Here's to showing as much ass as possible in 2020 y'all": a call to document all aspects of Appalachian sexuality, especially the more erotic or overtly sexual.[34] Other posts, like that of January 3, 2020 (figure 2), further emphasize the possibilities of sexually explicit queer content that the internet affords. This post depicts four queer people, some Appalachian and some Floridian, visiting a Waffle House (a cultural signifier of Appalachia and the South in general).[35] The four people are posing in front of the iconic Waffle House sign in various states of undress while three of these people eat waffles and pour maple syrup on Mamone, the former director of the project. While not as sexually explicit as the underwater post, the presence of half-naked bodies, messy food, and the public setting all work to challenge the respectable queer images that often appear in archives. The wide reach of the page's call for submissions enables facets of queer people's identities that do not fit current American hegemonic norms of gender, sexuality, or body types—a queer woman of color or a fat nonbinary person—to represent themselves. The Waffle House post, which depicts a group of nonbinary people and women who are not skinny, and which contains and references people of color, is an example of this representative range.

In addition to the wide range of genders, sexualities, races, and body types that appear in the Queer Appalachia Instagram archive, the account differentiates itself from conventional archives by making use of Instagram's tagging feature, which allows an account to imbed a link to another account. Many Queer Appalachia posts tag the accounts of rural queer people, radical political groups, or specific activist efforts that require attention (with the consent of the person who submitted the post). In doing so, Queer Appalachia constantly expands its archive to include not just a singular image, graphic, or video but entire accounts that show the lives and efforts of other queer-Appalachians. By tagging these other accounts, Queer Appalachia deepens their individual posts, illustrating that the objects in their archive necessarily include the lives and feelings of the object's creator. These links to other people's and groups' ways of life testify to the Instagram account's status as an "archive of feelings" that documents the highly ephemeral "lived experiences" and "cultural traces" attached to every queer object.[36] Moreover, through this tagging feature, the Queer Appalachia Instagram account begins to decentralize itself; a post that tags one queer user can link to a multitude of other similar accounts, which can link back to the Queer Appalachia Instagram account. There is no central hub of queer-Appalachian activity, only various pages linked by tags. Along with embodying Queer Appalachia's insistence on nonhierarchical archiving, this use of the tagging feature transforms the account from a digital record of queer-Appalachian experiences into the "floating signifier" that Halberstam describes—a highly mobile, adaptable, and constantly changing site of queer objects and emotions.[37]

Using Instagram as a means of queer archiving is not a flawless process, however. Despite the website's relative leniency toward gender and sexual expression in comparison to conventional state archives, vague "community guidelines" still often limit the full expression of LGBTQIA+ people.[38] Additionally, the relative anonymity of the internet, especially incredibly large Instagram accounts, can potentially lead to abuses of power and money, as people can send money to an individual or organization that may have dubious motives despite being outwardly progressive. This is particularly true for the Queer Appalachia Instagram account, as evidenced by the revelations made in an August 2020 *Washington Post* article by journalist Emma Copley Eisenberg.[39] In this article, Eisenberg alleges, using testimonies (both anonymous and otherwise) from people involved with the Queer Appalachia project, that Mamone mishandled large amounts of mutual money and used art in Queer Appalachia publications without properly paying or acknowledging the artists.

Along with the alleged theft of art and embezzling of money, one of the more distressing allegations against the Queer Appalachia project is the removal of critical comments on various posts by queer Black Appalachians.[40] The comments section of a post, like the tags and the post itself, is a critical space for preserving and documenting responses to the content within the post. Whether the comments include other queer-Appalachians posting stories that relate to the image, tagging others in their networks to look at the post, or criticizing the post or the account, these comments provide an additional dimension of the "feelings" that Cvetkovich describes—feelings that are almost entirely unique to the social media archival format. To delete or censor these comments, especially critical ones from queer Black Appalachians, is to reinforce the same racial and sexual gatekeeping that characterizes conventional archives under the control of conservative institutions.[41] In this way, the Queer Appalachia project Instagram archive ironically runs the risk of becoming almost identical to the current limited archives of Appalachia, with the gate opened slightly enough to include white queer-Appalachians.

However, just as the Queer Appalachia account can tag other accounts, expanding the scope of the archive, so too can these accounts tag Queer Appalachia, with it appearing on the main account's page, under the "tagged photos" tab. In the wake of Mamone and Queer Appalachia's alleged embezzlement, mistreatment of writers and artists, and the theft of artistic work, this tab has become a site of exposure, solidarity, and community, as more and more people begin to emerge and recount their stories of abuse. As a show of solidarity, many of the posts that reveal mistreatment by the Queer Appalachia project also reference the multitude of less popular or recently formed accounts that document queer experiences in Appalachia, tagging these accounts.[42] Much as the Queer Appalachia project, at its inception, sought to disrupt and decenter the control of hegemonic institutions (like corporations or governments) that are typically in control of conventional archives, so too are the personal testimonies and collective efforts of these numerous accounts decentering the Queer Appalachia project as the primary archive and the most popular voice of LGBTQIA+ life in the region.[43]

In this way, the digital archive that is the Queer Appalachia account, the posts in which the account is tagged, the comments to these posts, and the array of other accounts now gaining more visibility are not just a collective archive of queer-Appalachian experiences in general but the very specific experiences of queer-Appalachians and others as they relate to mistreatment at the hands of the Queer Appalachia project. The collective reckoning by various queer-Appalachian networks of the Queer Appalachia project *on* the project's account reinforces Cvetkovich's notion that shared experiences and "memory become a valuable historical resource."[44] The "feelings" within this archive of feelings thus expand to include the rage, sadness, frustration, hurt, and disappointment that surround this event.

Despite the many flaws in theory and practice with its early manifestations, the use of the internet and social digital organizing as a means to archive a wide range of Appalachian queer experiences still manages to improve upon or work around many (but not all) of the difficulties of accessibility and conservative sexual and racial politics that characterize conventional institutional archives. The Queer Appalachia Instagram account and the increased popularity of many other accounts signal the growing potential and legitimacy of digital archives for queer preservation. Future groups, queer or otherwise, looking to create a nonhierarchical, borderless archive can look to Queer Appalachia's ongoing attempt and failures as a model upon which to grow and expand.

The dominant metronormative narratives about queerness in Appalachia argue that queer people in Appalachia do not exist, and if they did they would most certainly be suffering. The Queer Appalachia project's social media archive (even with its many recent failures) pushes back against these narratives, asserting that LGBTQIA+ Appalachians *do* exist and that they navigate joy, suffering, survival, visibility, culture, and community on their *own* terms. In doing so, this unconventional archive constructs new models for queer archives in any geography. Not as tightly bound by the red tape and dominant moral ideals of local, state, and federal governments, a new approach to archiving becomes possible—one with the potential to emerge almost entirely from community funding, horizontal organization, mutual aid, and the wide range of the internet.

Appendix

Screenshot of @queerappalachia Instagram post appearing on December 31, 2019

Screenshot of @queerappalachia Instagram post appearing on January 3, 2020

NOTES

1   The simultaneous otherizing and romanticizing of Appalachia throughout
    history and the contemporary historical moment is readily visible in the dozens
    of "Trump Country" pieces written around the election of Donald Trump. These
    pieces place blame on an impoverished and allegedly backward Appalachia
    for the election of Donald Trump, while also reinforcing historically mythi-
    cal ideas about Appalachia. For examples of the "Trump Country" piece, see
    Lisa Lerer, "Once a Clinton Stronghold, Appalachia Now Trump Country," PBS,
    May 3, 2016, accessed October 8, 2021, https://www.pbs.org/newshour/nation/
    once-a-clinton-stronghold-appalachia-now-trump-country; Sam Levine, "This

County Gives a Glimpse at the America That Voted Trump into Office," HuffPost, November 18, 2016, accessed October 8, 2021, https://www.huffpost.com/entry/ mcdowell-county-trump_n_582f18dde4b030997bbefa0d; Larissa MacFarquhar, "In the Heart of Trump Country," *New Yorker*, October 10, 2016, accessed October 8, 2021, https://www.newyorker.com/magazine/2016/10/10/in-the-heart-of-trump-country; Paul Lewis, Tom Silverstone, and Adithya Sambamurthy, "Why the Poorest County in West Virginia Has Faith in Trump" (video), *Guardian*, October 13, 2016, accessed October 8, 2021, https://tinyurl.com/kxyb3tt7.

2   Like the "Trump Country" piece, J.D. Vance, *Hillbilly Elegy* (New York: HarperCollins, 2016) similarly depicts Appalachia as an inherently hostile region, while also fetishizing "bootstrap" narratives about individual escapes from poverty.

3   For many people inside and outside Appalachia, the most prominent examples of rural queerness are films like John Boorman's *Deliverance* or Ang Lee's *Brokeback Mountain*, in which queer people are either animalistic rapists (*Deliverance*) or entirely unable to have any meaningful queer relationships without melancholy and violent death (*Brokeback Mountain*). In both films, the takeaway is clear: LGBTQIA+ life and rural life do not mix.

4   Jack Halberstam, *In a Queer Time and Place: Transgender Bodies, Subcultural Lives* (New York: New York University Press, 2005), 36.

5   Ibid.

6   For example, historian John Howard notes in his book *Men Like That* that queer men in rural Mississippi "proved quite adept at maneuvering through hostile terrain" by altering their language and mannerisms based on their environment. By signaling their identity in this complex manner, many queer men were able to build "material and ideological spaces and thereby regularly found themselves in the company of like-minded souls." This "gay world" in heavily policed areas allows for a more nuanced approach to historical ideas of visibility; gay people could remain perfectly visible within the communal spaces that they have established, while continuing to pass within non-gay spaces; John Howard, *Men Like That: A Southern Queer History* (Chicago: University of Chicago Press, 1999), xiv.

7   Carly Thomsen, "In Plain(s) Sight," in *Queering the Countryside: New Frontiers in Rural Queer Studies*, ed. Mary L. Gray, Colin R. Johnson, and Brian J Gilley, 244–66 (New York: New York University Press, 2016), 249.

8   In this case, "self-aggrandizement" refers to the ways in which the liberal authors of "Trump Country" pieces scapegoat Appalachia for the election of Donald Trump, enabling these writers and their readers to absolve wealthy corporations and politicians of blame and pass that blame onto Appalachia. This scapegoating allows these writers and readers to take the blame off of themselves, feel superior to the Appalachians they condemn, and remain complacent, without addressing any of the deeper problems of capitalist exploitation (and related problems like racism, sexism, and homophobia) that better explain the current state of American politics. For examples of this self-aggrandizement, see the examples of "Trump Country" pieces listed in note 1 above.

9 "West Virginia and Regional History Center: Collections," West Virginia and Regional History Center, West Virginia University, accessed October 8, 2021, https://wvrhc.lib.wvu.edu/collections.

10 Barbara Ellen Smith, "Beyond the Mountains: The Paradox of Women's Place in Appalachian History," in *NWSA Journal* 11, no. 3 (Autumn 1999): 1–17.

11 Ibid.

12 Chad Berry, Phillip J. Obermiller, and Shaunna L. Scott, *Studying Appalachian Studies: Making the Path by Walking* (Chicago: University of Illinois Press, 2015), 26.

13 The following is not an exhaustive list but still represents a sizeable portion of the current published scholarship regarding queer people in Appalachia: Jeffrey C. Cawood, "Out in Appalachia: Leaving the Closet in the Mountains" (master's thesis, Morehead State University, 2018), accessed October 8, 2021, https://scholarworks.moreheadstate.edu/msu_theses_dissertations/130; Mathias J. Detamore, *Queer Appalachia: Toward Geographies of Possibility* (PhD diss., University of Kentucky Doctoral Dissertations, 2010), accessed October 8, 2021, https://uknowledge.uky.edu/gradschool_diss/57; Rachel Garringer, *The Republic of Fabulachia: Queer Visions for a Post-Coal Appalachian Future* (PhD diss., University of North Carolina, 2017), accessed October 8, 2021, https://cdr.lib.unc.edu/concern/dissertations/c534fp36b; Amy Michelle Jordan, "Those Who Choose to Stay: Narrating the Rural Appalachian Queer Experience" (master's thesis: University of Tennessee Knoxville, 2015), accessed October 8, 2021, https://trace.tennessee.edu/utk_gradthes/3375; Jeff Mann, Maggie and Julia Watts, *LGBTQ Fiction and Poetry from Appalachia* (Morgantown:West Virginia University Press, 2019); Jeff Mann, *Loving Mountains, Loving Men* (Athens: Ohio University Press, 2005).

14 On storytelling, see Hillery Glasby, Sherrie Gradin, and Rachael Ryerson, eds., *Storytelling in Queer Appalachia: Imagining and Writing the Unspeakable Other* (Morgantown: West Virginia University Press, 2020).

15 Throughout this chapter, I refer to academic archives as institutional, state, or "official" archives due to the collaboration between state governments, academic institutions, and public understandings on what is "official." There are a handful of queer archives tied to universities throughout the country that do important work in preserving and documenting the queer experience, such as the ONE Archive at the University of Southern California. However, there is no dedicated academic archive of queer-Appalachian history and culture, and many universities, Appalachian or otherwise, are just beginning to form LGBTQIA+ archives.

16 Ann Cvetkovich, *An Archive of Feelings* (Durham, NC: Duke University Press, 2003), 7.

17 Ibid.

18 Halberstam, *In a Queer Time and Place*, 169–70.

19 Ibid., 170.

20 Some of the questions specifically related to archiving include: What, in your opinion, are the best ways that a queer person can preserve their experiences? Why do you see archives are particularly important for queer people, especially queer-Appalachians?

21   Nan A. Boyd, "Talking about Sex," in *Bodies of Evidence*, ed. Nan A. Boyd and Horacio R. Ramirez. (London: Oxford University Press, 2012), 110.

22   After a 2020 article in the *Washington Post* by Emma Copley Eisenberg revealed that Mamone allegedly engaged in the embezzlement of hundreds of thousands of dollars and used art by Black and Indigenous artists without crediting them, an anonymous Black West Virginian activist took control of the account with a renewed emphasis on reparations and accountability.

23   Maxwell Cloe, "Mamone Oral History," transcript of an oral history conducted 2019 by Maxwell Cloe, Monroe Summer Research project College of William and Mary, Williamsburg, 2019.

24   Ibid.

25   Philip Kennicott, "The National Archives Used to Stand for Independence. That Mission Has Been Compromised," *Washington Post*, January 18, 2020, accessed October 8, 2021, https://tinyurl.com/6uvnnhwn.

26   "In order to tell the story of the cross-dresser or the transgender subject, the biographer must convince herself that her own life is normal, beyond reproach, honest"; Halberstam, *In a Queer Time and Place*, 59.

27   See historian Nan Boyd's comments on "permissible speech"; Nan A. Boyd, "Talking about Sex," 110.

28   Cloe, "Mamone Oral History."

29   In February 2020, for example, Mamone announced multiple guest curators for the account, all of whom were queer Black Southerners and Appalachians. The caption to the February 14 post that announced these guests reads as follows: "We got some special community members that are helping us curate February's feed. @oppressedjuice, @gemynii, @lilbearboi & @azzan.theartist are going to help us explore queer Black-Appalachian/Southern Art, Culture & Community ALL month long!"

30   John Howard, "Digital Oral History and the Limits of Gay Sex," in *Queering the Countryside: New Frontiers in Rural Queer Studies*, ed. Mary L. Gray, Colin R. Johnson, and Brian Joseph Gilley (New York: New York University Press, 2016), 326.

31   Posts on the account are generally submitted by queer-Appalachians and then posted after review by Mamone and others.

32   Ibid., 329.

33   Maxwell Cloe, "Jon Coleman Oral History," transcript of an oral history conducted 2019 by Maxwell Cloe, Monroe Summer Research project, College of William and Mary, Williamsburg, 2019.

34   Queer Appalachia post, Instagram, December 31, 2019, accessed October 8, 2021, https://www.instagram.com/p/B6wsWMPlTAm.

35   Alan Blinder, "Portrait of the South, Served Up One Waffle House Order at a Time," *New York Times*, April 25, 2018, accessed October 8, 2021, https://www.nytimes.com/2018/04/25/us/waffle-house-american-south.html.

36   Cvetkovich, *An Archive of Feelings*, 9.

37   Halberstam, *In a Queer Time and Place*, 169.

38   Instagram's "community guidelines" restrict nudity and sexual activity with the following prohibition: "for a variety of reasons, we don't allow nudity on

Instagram. This includes photos, videos, and some digitally-created content that show sexual intercourse, genitals, and close-ups of fully-nude buttocks. It also includes some photos of female nipples." Such vague prohibitions, especially those against "female nipples," do not account for the wide range of human body types that exist. How would these community guidelines handle transgender men before and after surgery? Transgender women before and after surgery? By relying on these ill-defined guidelines, Instagram constructs gender and sexuality solely in biological terms, excluding those who do not fall within those strict scientific lines.

39   Emma Copley Eisenberg, "A Popular Instagram Account Raises Funds for LGBTQ People in Appalachia. It's Not Clear Where Those Donations Go," *Washington Post*, August 3, 2020, accessed October 8, 2021, https://tinyurl.com/549sahht.

40   Eisenberg writes that Shane Hicks, a Black trans Appalachian man, "routinely left comments on QA posts criticizing content that he saw as anti-Black or excluding of people of color. But his critical comments were quickly deleted, he says."

41   Though not identical, the erasure of critical queer Black-Appalachian comments is analogous to the censorship of anti-Trump protest signs in the National Archives. In both cases, dissent against anti-Blackness and white supremacy results in the total erasure of such dissent from a popular archive.

42   Some of these alternative accounts include: @biblebeltqueers, @radicalkindred, @marxinthemountains, @appalachianfeministcoalition, @queerfarmecologies, and @queerlifeappalachia. This is not to mention the many personal accounts of queer-Appalachian people documenting their experiences.

43   Another important, though unresolved, aspect of this scandal is the momentary takeover of the Queer Appalachia Instagram account by an anonymous queer Black organizer in Appalachia. This takeover took place in early August and was announced through an Instagram post that the account was going to be "decolonized" and handed over to a collective of queer-Appalachian BIPOC. Within two weeks, however, Mamone reclaimed this account, leaving the future of the project uncertain.

44   Cvetkovich, *An Archive of Feelings*, 8.

ABOUT THE AUTHOR

Maxwell Cloe (they/he) is an oral historian and MA student in American Studies at William and Mary. Their research centers on LGBTQIA+ histories and cultures in the Appalachian Mountains, particularly artistic and archival networks. They are additionally interested in oral history methodology, twentieth-century Southern literature, environmental activism, and radical labor movements. Their dissertation project focuses on the intersections of LGBTQIA+ Appalachian art and environmental justice.

Lessons for the Long Term: One Story of the Queer Appalachia Platform

Rachel Casiano Hernandez

I started following Queer Appalachia (QA) in 2017. It was billed as a zine and Instagram page documenting the lives and activism of LGBTQIA+ people in and from Appalachia and the South. It was one of the first times I felt like I could be proud about where I was born and raised, and not like I had to either defend or apologize for it. It was a respite from the alienating experiences of living in the Northeast (where I had years before trained myself out of saying "y'all"), and it was grounding to learn about other Southern and Appalachian queer people when I had grown up thinking I was one of two lesbians in my high school. I learned about new radical political projects and met people—some of whom had grown up near me who I'd never known. I made the connections of different struggles across different lands—like extractive economies in both West Virginia and Puerto Rico—and how people were resisting through solidarity. Somewhere along the years, I must have known that QA was mostly white, but as a casual follower it was hard to know who was involved.

I began to have my doubts about QA around 2019, though I can't pin down exactly when. I don't know if it was because it got more popular in big coastal cities, or because time and energy were being spent on different offshoot projects, but the tone of the account had changed. There was more gatekeeping—like the post about how to "correctly" pronounce Appalachia (which I apparently say "incorrectly," despite having been born and raised in western Maryland). There was a pronounced anti-urban hostility under the guise of combating metronormativity—apparently if you don't think Mothman on a gender-neutral bathroom sign is cute, you're a white New York hipster. There were posts by QA and comments strangely valorizing nativism and positioning the ability of one's family to stay in one place intergenerationally as a virtue... even though immigrants are an increasing presence in Appalachia and even when the people who touted this line benefited from settler-colonialism.

As someone with family from Puerto Rico who lives in New York City now, I felt like I didn't have the credibility to push back on some of these ideas (and when I did, comments would get restricted or deleted). I didn't fit the purity test that was being established. I watched discussions in the comments about whether Pittsburgh "counts" as Appalachia or whether Black and Brown people living in urban poverty are privileged, and I couldn't help but think: Who wins from these kinds of conversations? Who wins when we shut people out instead of bridging difference toward shared struggle? Why aren't the moderators saying anything? As QA seemed to position itself and all of Appalachia and the South as "anti–New York" and anti-diaspora, it felt increasingly difficult to engage and relate. This was no longer for me, but I accepted that not everything has to be, and I continued to donate to its projects.

All of that is to say, the *Washington Post* article and response from QA didn't surprise me. Something in me was seeing cracks already. The primacy of one person in an alleged collective and the dual silencing and profit extracted from Black community members troubled me more than the financials around a coat drive. We've seen this sort of thing before, over and over again with all/majority-white organizations: seemingly small normalized misuses of power setting the groundwork for larger violations, with the justification that "it's for a good cause"; conspiracy theorizing if the source of damning information is considered suspect; leaving a mess for smaller organizations or less well-known (often nonwhite) people to try to clean up. I feel guilty and frustrated that I didn't know about this harm being done, and that capitalist media had to open the floodgates of people's stories for QA's casual followers. I expect some shit to get messy with DIY projects, but if they'd been transparent about the messiness, it would still have been possible to maintain trust.

Other people have put forth suggestions about what to do in the short term about QA: de/replatform to center radical Black and Indigenous voices; make it an actual collective; financial transparency; reparations to people who were harmed. As I write this, the platform has changed hands to a radical Black activist, with the promise of transitioning to multiple administrators. I look forward to these changes.

But I wonder what broader lessons we should be taking for the long term. Part of what was appealing to me about QA (well, besides feeling seen and spoken to initially) was the idea of an information hub and being able to learn about many different projects in one place. But I wonder now how useful that is if the container of information itself has a racist bias or doesn't allow for multiple narratives. Convenience has its costs, whether it's the convenience of a central hub or the "convenience" of a flattened narrative of a singular queer Appalachia. We should try to resist convenience. We should be critical of a movement that relies on branding—that's usually the first step to monopolizing and whitewashing a struggle. We should trust our instincts if something seems off. If something seems too easy or good to be true, it probably is. We should be critical of the idea that a shared identity is by definition a shared struggle. We should be wary of people appointing themselves as leaders or heroes on our behalf.

Ultimately, though, we should remember that movement-building in Appalachia existed before the Queer Appalachia platform and will exist long after it's gone. There were Klan rallies when I was in high school, but there were counterprotesters who got in their faces and doxed them and eventually drove them out. There was also an anarchist infoshop in my town (short-lived, and just one bookshelf, but still!), something that I had forgotten until finding the QA platform. There was a little tour circuit for local shows. There were people driving out the Nazi punks who tried to come. When I go visit my parents, no one calls the cops if I speak Spanish with my mom in public. I barely see any Confederate flags anymore. These changes aren't an accident, and they didn't come out of nowhere. Power comes from people building relationships and coalitions and fighting for their space.

ABOUT THE AUTHOR
Rachel Casiano Hernandez is a big gay lefty DiaspoRican acupuncturist who makes zines and overthinks everything.

The "Wyrd" and Wonderful Queerness of Appalachian Oral History in Theory and Practice

Matthew R. Sparks

Oral history is my vocation, and, retrospectively, I hardly had much of a choice in the matter. In fact, you could say that I was quite literally born into the art. I am the latest link in a chain of family history, folklore, and, of course, "haint tales" (ghost stories) beginning at the latest with my earliest ancestor's arrival in the Appalachian mountains of Southeastern Kentucky. Some of my earliest memories involve being told these stories in various settings by my grandparents, parents, extended family, and neighbors, and retelling them to riveted audiences whenever I had the opportunity. However, I did not always understand or appreciate the significance of oral history as a method for Appalachian queers to access and engage with the past.

From my Appalachian childhood to my queer adulthood in academia, the oral histories I inherited were never merely irrelevant echoes from a past long forgotten. On the contrary, they provided a context for my identity and a mechanism for its transformation, a method of actively interpreting and engaging in dialogue with my history at the personal, familial, and regional level, and, finally, a means of transmitting historical, cultural, and folk knowledge to future generations of Appalachians and the world at large.

In this exploration of queer-Appalachian oral history in theory and practice, I argue that oral history is perhaps one of the most easily accessible and relevant forms of history not only for queer-Appalachians but for queer groups in general. I hope to identify what I consider to be the three key characteristics of Appalachian queer oral history as a discipline that distinguishes it from other forms of oral history:

1.   Historically contextualizing the subjective experiences of Appalachian queers.[1]

2.	Providing a traditional medium for facilitating historical reflection, dialogue, and reconciliation from within Appalachian culture.[2]
3.	Creating a unique archive for Appalachian queers to form the basis of future work within the field of Appalachian Studies.[3]

With this short analysis of some work I and others have done on Appalachian oral history, I hope to demonstrate the revitalizing potential of queer oral histories in the region and inspire others to document and engage with our living historical tradition, as we continue to define our malleable future.

Oral History Theory, the "Wyrd," and the Shaping of the Appalachian Worldview

In the 2019 collection *Appalachian Reckoning*, Dr. Edward Karshner, associate professor of English at Robert Morris University, addresses the metaphysical importance of destiny, or the realm of past possibilities, in Appalachian culture, using an ancient Anglo-Saxon concept, the *wyrd*. Following Karshner's train of thought in connecting the wyrd to the role of oral histories in Appalachia, I hope to expand upon Karshner's analysis by illustrating how Appalachian queer oral histories provide a unique means of engaging queer historical subjects within the process of historical interpretation and transmission.[4]

In recent years, oral histories have illuminated the historical experiences of groups of people (often marginalized) living without written documentation.[5] Whereas the first oral histories of the modern era dealt with the lives of the working class, the rise of queer theory and analysis has enabled oral history methods to access not only the historical memory of queer folk, but also to approach an understanding of lived reality as subjectively experienced by queers from all walks of life.[6] Appalachian queer oral histories reveal the contours not only of a modern region, its people, and its history but also the formative cultural and environmental influences that have characterized Appalachian queer identity in the past.[7] Beyond queer theory, in deconstructing Appalachian queerness through oral histories, we can approach a greater understanding of the Appalachian region and its people as a whole by analyzing the interplay between traditional norms and perceived queer or subversive elements in the society.

In the Appalachian context, where access to educational and economic opportunities has historically been scarce, oral traditions encompassing folklore, family history (genealogy), and life histories have thrived. In addition to offering historical perspectives "from below" that cannot be obtained from national or archival sources, Karshner argues that Appalachian oral histories possess a multidimensional character, which facilitates the development of a unique worldview (or *cosmovision*).[8] Karshner defines this multidimensional character using the old Norse term "wyrd", as "that which has been laid down," meaning the set of folklore and oral knowledge encompassing past events and determining future ones.[9] According to Karshner, when these wyrd beliefs are transmitted, they serve as tools to manifest history, by broadly delineating the realm of possibilities contained within it.[10] To the recipient, these transmitted tales constitute one's "luck" or "hamingja" as Karshner would describe it. Hamingja then, is not merely our own inherited embodied knowledge, but our ability to engage with and transmit it to our posterity.[11]

In my own journey as an Appalachian oral historian, I have realized that our past, in the form of our wyrd body of oral histories, does in fact have the potential to radically redefine ourselves and our region.

My Wyrd Appalachian Upbringing: Oral History and the Development of My Queer Identity

In my childhood, my grandmother would tell me many stories of her childhood on Cutshin Creek in Leslie County, Kentucky. Among my favorites were "haint tales" involving spirits that would jump on the back of horses and frighten their riders in an area known as the "Wolf Pen," and, of course, tales of witchcraft and faith healing among my distant kin. Much like Karshner describes, although I didn't know it at the time, these tales were my "hamingja": a body of inherited lore that instilled within my young Appalachian self a remarkable sense of reverence for the mystery, and the magical potentiality, that lay not only within myself, but also within my region. As I grew up and came to terms with my Appalachian and later queer identity, I returned to these stories as a documentarian and an oral historian. This time, however, I applied a critical eye to these narratives. What I was able to find by putting these narratives into conversation with other Leslie County oral histories, queer oral histories (such as the Country Queers Project), and other ethnobotanical sources, was quite revelatory.[12] Confirming what many scholars of Appalachia have recently brought to the table, these oral histories seem to provide evidence that Appalachia has historically acted as a site of syncretism between European, Indigenous, and African cultures. This is particularly true with regard to faith healing practices, herbal lore, and belief in magic/witchcraft.

In my article "The 'Charm Doctors' of Leslie County: Oral Histories of Male Witches, Midwives, and Faith Healers in Leslie County, Kentucky 1878–1978," I examine the oral legacy of three representatives of this social role in detail, offering several points for further analysis.[13] The cases of George Joseph, John Maggard, and Matt Gray discussed here illustrate how the wyrd can provide a dynamic foundation for developing Appalachian queer identity by informing one's cultural cosmovision and linking the present with the past.

George Joseph, a local herb doctor who lived in Leslie County in the late nineteenth and early twentieth century, was believed by many in the county to be a witch in the classical sense of the term. Oral histories tell of him being able to cure illnesses with herbs and incantations, cast spells to transform into an animal, move livestock by magical means, and even prophesize and predict the future. Below are two popular narratives concerning George that I heard as a child, recounted here by Mallie Sizemore and Tena Baker Dean.[14]

Bewitching the Butter

> That old man George Joseph, yeah, well he went around a lot to people. He was really old, and he didn't really have a home of his own I don't reckon much. He just went to different places and stayed. He would come to my daddy's and mother's and stay all night. People told he had witched people and all. And he came to my mother's once and daddy's, and he asked my mother to let him churn. She said she didn't have any milk. He said well it don't take milk for me to make a big bowl of butter! But she didn't let him churn. He said he could make a bowl of butter churning water, but mother didn't let him churn. One of the neighbors said they did, but they sure wouldn't eat the butter! They were afraid to eat it!
>
> —Mallie Sizemore[15]

The Cow on the Top of the Barn

I spoke with an aunt today, and she said that some people thought him to be a witch, because he would tell them things and they would happen. My grandma said that he was a very religious man and was a preacher. She said he was a good person. He told a man once that was going to sell a cow that was not a good cow to someone, and he said you can't do wrong and get by with it. They talked a little while, and George told him you want sell that cow tomorrow. The man got up the next morning. The people that was going to buy it was there. They went to the barn, and the cow was on top of the barn on the roof. George came along and said, I told you, you cannot do wrong and get by with it. Needless to say, he didn't sell the cow, and George told him the cow will be down shortly. Sure enough, that evening it was in the field.

—Tena Baker Dean[16]

John B. Maggard, a contemporary of George Joseph, was described by the citizens of Leslie County in more glowing terms as a faith healer, gunsmith, and farmer, who was said to possess the gift of the "healing hands." John was reported to be able to remove cancers and warts by reciting two Bible verses and laying his hands on the afflicted area. Furthermore, he was called upon frequently to cancel the spells of George Joseph, according to some sources. Below is a letter from his niece, Martha Maggard, requesting his services.

May 31, 1864
Mr. John Maggard,
Dear Unkie, after my best respecks, I can inform you that my sister Susannah Creech has a canser on the left side or edge of her tongue about the size of a five-cent piece, red around the edge and of a yellow mattered color in the middle, and I have herd that you cold take them away, and I want you to try your skill on this so no more but remains,
Yours till death,
Martha Maggard[17]

Much like Karshner, these stories sustained my backwoods childhood, filling the people and the mountains in Leslie County with a sense of wyrd possibility. Demonstrated by the almost tangible reality of these individuals, proven by my grandmother's oral testimony, and those of others in the county.

While the realities of growing up queer in Appalachia in the early and mid-2000s was far less magical than the wyrd potentialities of the Appalachian yesteryear I grew up on, in my late teens I became acquainted with other, more modern accounts of individuals in Leslie County who had fully utilized their hamingja to wyrd effect.

Matt Gray, unlike our past two subjects, lived well into the twentieth century, and can be considered a contemporary example of the wyrd power of traditional Appalachian healing knowledge. Our information about his life is preserved by an extensive oral history interview conducted by Dale Deaton in 1978. In his own words, Matt Gray was trained to be a mountain doctor by both of his parents (of Cherokee and English ancestry), who also functioned as mountain doctors.[18]

From the interview, it is clear that Matt Gray was both a skilled midwife and herb doctor, having delivered numerous children and treated numerous illnesses using only practical experience. His only tools were household instruments and medicinal herbs, and his only education was his on-the-job experience and traditional knowledge received from his parents.

Gray first explained how he used a tea made of boiled black gum tree bark or red pepper leaves to "raise misery," or induce labor, in an expectant mother. Gray then described in detail how he delivered a baby at home, using only homemade instruments and articles sterilized with olive oil, rubbing alcohol, and peroxide. After waiting until the labor pains were four to five minutes apart, Gray proceeded to explain how he prepared the mother by placing her on a pillow and sterilizing his hands. He then delivered the infant when the baby's head came into sight.

In addition to his "inherited" skills as a midwife, Matt Gray also inherited an extensive tradition of herbal knowledge and treatments for a wide variety of illnesses.[19] Nearly all of these cures were derived from the Cherokee tradition,[20] with some of the more noteworthy including:

Natural Pregnancy Test: yellow dogwood (most likely *Cornus florida*) tea (will induce purging in the mother if she is pregnant)
Fever: three inches of dried rattlesnake steeped in water
Hives: deer's tongue (*Liatris odoratissima*)
Measles: tea made of boiled sheep dung

Shingles: blood of a black animal (cat or chicken) applied to shingles
Cold: burr vine (most likely *Galium aparine*), blue and yellow top
stickweed (*Ambrosia artmisiifolia*) ginseng (*Panax quinquefolius*)
Pneumonia: dried rattlesnake
Constipation: elm root (*Ulmus americana*)
Headache: mustard green poultice (*Brassica juncea*)
Colic: blow tobacco in a spoon of breast milk, give to the infant
Upset stomach: wintergreen (*Gaultheria procumbens*)[21]

In terms of both his role as a healer and as a recipient of traditional healing knowledge, we see in Matt Gray a continuation of the Appalachian role of the "charm" doctor: a composite social role whose knowledge of the "wyrd" enables him to affect healing or magical powers for the greater good of society. Apart from cultural documentation, what can we gain from putting these oral histories in conversation with contemporary oral histories and the modern day issues of queer-Appalachians?

Modern Appalachian Queer Oral Histories: Identity and Reconciliation

In the summer of 2017, I authored a piece for a two-part series in the *Activist History Review* centered on exploring the intersections of poverty, gender, sexuality, and whiteness in the rural American South. This piece, "The Unsettling of Appalachia," sparked several conversations among fellow Appalachians, writers, and scholars about the complex subject of identity in modern Appalachia. In this piece, I presented the thesis that in failing to develop a cohesive modern identity for ourselves as Appalachians (on our own terms) our identity has continued to be defined for us by the hegemonic American cultural paradigm currently in power.[22] Thus, Appalachia has been, and continues to be, a control group or a barometer of sorts "against which social progress in this country can be measured." The issue of identity is critical for contemporary Appalachians to address, as it leaves us as peripheral nonagents, unable to truly participate in the current cultural and political discourse in a real and meaningful sense.

Inspired by the responses and seeking to further examine the questions generated by this piece, I began a small Appalachian oral history project based out of my native Leslie County in which I interviewed eight self-identifying queer individuals from the area. All interviews were conducted with the informed consent of the interviewees on a voluntary basis, under the condition of anonymity. All interviewees self-identified as queer and were between the ages of twenty-four and forty-five. In this section of this chapter, I will share some of the more pressing insights gained from this oral history project and hope that in doing so to demonstrate the profound implications and possibilities of wyrd oral history for reconciling Appalachian and queer identities.[23]

When asked about what it means to identify as an Appalachian, all interviewees expressed a great pride in their historical and cultural heritage, while acknowledging the "shapeshifting" nature of the region, the conflict between modernity and traditionalism that has shaped their identity formation (as an Appalachian). One in particular acknowledged Appalachia's role as a "mirror" of the country, while another suggested that a focus on Appalachia's historic virtues of resilience, ingenuity, and self-reliance should serve as models for constructing a modern Appalachian identity. To extrapolate, as a mirror, Appalachia reflects an "Otherized" or distorted vision of the outside viewer, which, in turn, can provide an outlet for self-reflection for the rest of the country at large. For example, depending on one's political philosophy, some may choose to view Appalachia as a source of religious fundamentalism, racism, and cultural degeneracy, while ignoring the structural inequality, labor exploitation, and underdevelopment of the region. On the other hand, some may view Appalachia as the negative outcome of failed progressive social programs initiated by the "War on Poverty." Both views are fundamentally incorrect, as by its own nature, the mirror is more than the perception of the viewers reflection. To digress from this extended analogy, if self-reflection in Appalachia could contribute to a broader understanding of what it means to be Appalachian in the twenty-first century, oral history, particularly among queer-Appalachians, could certainly help to facilitate such internal dialogue.

Following this note, when asked if they consider Appalachia to be a queer region, all also agreed that it is a region of queer interests, by virtue of its otherness from hegemonic American culture, its role as a mirror/ social barometer, and, more recently, its status as a place of refuge for those seeking a more natural, communitarian, alternative mode of living from urban life. One interviewee in particular noted that while he would not describe it as an overall queer region, it is a region with a set of queer issues unique to its culture that need to be addressed.

I then asked the interviewees to describe how they understand gender roles historically and at present as they operate in Appalachia. All agreed that gender roles have been historically rigid in the region, largely for economic reasons, with men being the primary breadwinners and women supervising the care of the home and children. Interestingly, two interviewees in particular noted the matriarchal aspects of Appalachian family/clan groups, in which strong "mamaw" figures tend to play powerful advisory roles. One noted that this phenomenon is undergoing something of a revival with a renewed interest in the Appalachian "granny witch" role and the lore surrounding it. Another noted that due to an increased focus on education and economic necessity, female gender roles have rapidly changed in the region and will largely continue to do so, while masculine gender roles have remained static.

When I began to delve into questions related to identifying as queer and Appalachian, the responses became much more varied and layered in complexity. While all interviewees expressed no issue with identifying as Appalachian and queer at the personal level, they each identified several cultural and political barriers that made it difficult for them to identify with broader Appalachian culture. Three interviewees explained that this was particularly difficult when engaging in current political discourse, all articulating that they feel torn between supporting the political left due to their social progressivism and the political right due to their obligations to family and the local economy. Another argued that the political indifference on both sides of the political spectrum to Appalachian issues in general had made them mostly politically apathetic.

Two interviewees in particular noted that the overall "queerness" of the Appalachian region in the above described sense made it much easier to reconcile their own queerness with themselves. One, however, observed that Appalachia's stereotypical image as being backward, ignorant, and bigoted made it difficult for themselves to identify as Appalachian.

On the subject of larger challenges facing the Appalachian queer community, all interviewed parties expressed that familial acceptance (at least with their primary parents/guardians/caregivers) was not the most pressing issue within the Appalachian queer community as they understood it at present. In fact, several agreed that the overwhelming lack of community support and resources for queer-Appalachians was the greatest threat to the flourishing of queer communities in the region. Frustratingly, as one interviewee pointed out, the endurance of traditional male gender roles in the region has made it difficult, if not impossible, for queer males in particular to thrive in the area.

In concluding the interviews, I asked participants to relay their thoughts on the future of queer culture in Appalachia in light of other, potentially larger, problems the region currently faces. Only two of eight interviewees seemed optimistic that the region will continue to evolve in its acceptance of queer-Appalachians as part of the broader Appalachian community, though all agreed that solving the identity crisis facing Appalachians as a whole is a crucial step in increasing political participation in the region. One interviewee observed:

> At present, there is little in the way of an authentically Appalachian identity, as it has largely been subsumed by a broader "Southern" identity. This identity, with its strong ties to the religious right, has come to dominate the cultural and political landscape of Appalachia. In this environment, LGBTQ+ Appalachians are largely ignored, as LGBTQ+ issues are considered to be the domain of the opposite political camp. This places pressure on young LGBTQ+ people to leave the area, contributing to the loss of the intellectual and cultural resources that could help to address Appalachia's problems. I believe that if Appalachia is to be saved, then reconciliation with its LGBTQ+ population, among others, will be necessary.

Though many are pessimistic that much needed changes in the area will actually occur, some interviewees drew attention to the fact that many artists in the area are beginning to incorporate reflections on Appalachian identity in their work, perhaps suggesting that, as a culture, we are beginning the discourse necessary to facilitate change. One interviewee emphasized the importance of voluntarism in the region as a means to consolidate disparate groups in Appalachia as another source for optimism. Another rearticulated that a redefinition of traditional gender roles is essential for fostering a community in which queer individuals can thrive.

Although this oral history project is still ongoing, others, such as Rachel Garringer's "Country Queers" multimedia digital oral history project, provide additional insights from Southeastern Kentucky queer folk that supplement my own observations.

Take the case of Ivy (Country Queers), from neighboring Perry County, Kentucky, who was born in my hometown of Hyden and raised in the city of Viper. While articulating similar concerns about social conservatism, religion, and acceptance in Appalachia, she agrees that queerness and Appalachian society are not altogether incompatible and can, in fact, coexist harmoniously:

> In some ways, I think growing up where I did made it easier, and made it better, because people really knew who I was, and knew where I was coming from. I recently, so Vicco is a really small town, less than 400 people, um, that's close to Viper, and they recently passed a Fairness Ordinance. They have an openly gay mayor in Vicco, I mean it's yeah. It's really, it's this strange little pocket, of like progressiveness. But, um, I recently wrote this piece about Vicco for this blog that I worked for, before I was working at MACED. And um, just sort of talked about how in small communities like this people are supportive of other people, because you're in this small space and you know these people, it's not like a complete stranger. And it's hard to look at someone that you have grown up with and you've known all your life, and sort of shun this person, when you know who they are and you love this person.[24]

When asked about how she reconciles her identity as a queer with her identity as an Appalachian, Ivy comments that she sees no conflict in the two aspects of herself and is always proud to be a queer-Appalachian:

> It's always at the same time. It's always at the same time. Because that's those are both such huge parts of who I am that I can't separate those, so I think like, being proud of either one of those things, is being proud of the other. That's really sort of like vague and mystical, but, yeah I think um, you know I'm really proud, always to be an Appalachian.[25]

Ivy's comment here is telling. In this day and age, in which the cultures and traditions of Appalachia, though strong, are increasingly threatened, the endurance of our values, traditions, stories, and rugged way of life does take on a wyrd mystique.

The takeaway from the interviews, for me, is that for modern Appalachian queers, there is no fundamental identity crisis in being queer and Appalachian. Rather, certain social stigmas related to patriarchal cultural norms, religion, and family dynamics, and, by extension, the lack of family and social support, play larger roles in whether or not

Appalachian queers can thrive in their home regions. As we have seen with Ivy's account, the strength of familial and communal bonds can influence Appalachian queers positively in their decisions to remain as active parts of their communities.

Although challenges will persist for the region, this sampling of interview responses indicates that Appalachia is certainly a region of unique queer interests, with reconciliation between queer and Appalachian identity viewed as a possibility at both the individual and communal level. This reconciliation, I would argue, is partially made possible by our strong oral traditions, our inherent "wyrdness," which both helps us to understand our past and can pave the way for our future.

Conclusion: The "Wyrd" as Prologue—Oral History and the Future of Queer Appalachia

In Appalachia, though we lack much in the way of "progress" by American standards, our stories, and our wyrdness, continue to play a relevant role in all of our lives. In the current social and political climate, Appalachia continues to deal with much of the same economic and cultural stagnation we have been dealing with since the beginning of the so-called War on Poverty in 1964. Though cultural and sexual minorities have always been a part of the fabric of Appalachian life, we continue to face challenges related to participating as thriving members of our communities, in addition to the larger infrastructural and developmental problems faced by Appalachians in the twenty-first century. For too long, our voices have been silenced in favor of a dominant narrative of "Appalachianness" that does not accurately reflect the on-the-ground realities in the region. Creating our own histories and our own archives and ultimately integrating them within the larger framework of Appalachian history will be necessary to affect the much needed social and political change in the region. Engaging with our wyrd nature through oral history, I argue, is one of the best ways to facilitate this process, and, ultimately, achieve cultural integration.

Despite being one of the oldest forms of historical memory, oral histories are a form of history nearly unmatched in their subversive potential in the context of traditional national histories. They give voice to voiceless, marginalized, and overlooked historical actors. They are performative, multidimensional, and have the somewhat shamanic ability to engage their audiences in dialogues with the wyrd past.

Furthermore, they impress upon the recipient the burden of conveying the knowledge forward, expanding upon and maintaining the collective knowledge that will become the wyrd of a future generation. Although carrying this knowledge may be a burden, the living oral tradition in Appalachia is certainly our collective hamingja, as Karshner so eloquently put it. It grants us the awareness of the wyrd from our inherited knowledge so as to shape our individual and collective identity.

In providing this analysis of oral history in theory and practice at both the individual and collective level, I hope I have demonstrated how queer-Appalachians have, and can continue to, draw upon our wyrd oral histories to achieve the communal and cultural reconciliation needed to ensure the flourishing of our societies. The queer-Appalachian oral histories I have examined here have very accurately described our acute feelings of otherness, and the lack of support we feel from our communities. Oral histories involving not only shamanic healing but also individuals participating in roles considered to be atypical for gendered practices at the time (such as midwifery) can provide a cultural foundation of possibility or the wyrd, from which we can begin to analyze and reintegrate the queer aspect of Appalachian culture with our modern condition.

In short, not only is Appalachia currently a region of uniquely queer interests, but, as one of my interviewees observed, it always has been. If we are to negotiate our identity in a future that is not only postindustrial but sustainable in the true sense of the word, we must come to terms with reintegrating queer identity with the wyrdness of old Appalachia. Oral history narratives offer a uniquely Appalachian and uniquely queer way of achieving this integration; as we navigate past coal and into an uncertain future, the wyrd possibilities of our past can guide us toward finding our place and thriving within Appalachia, as we have done in the past.

NOTES

1   Alessandro Portelli, "What Makes Oral History Different?" in *Oral History, Oral Culture, and Italian Americans*, ed. Luisa Del Giudice (New York: Palgrave Macillan, 2009), 21–30.

2   Lynn Abrams, *Oral History Theory* (New York: Routledge, 2016).

3   Ibid.

4   Edward Karshner, "These Stories Sustain Me: The Wyrd-Ness of My Appalachia," in *Appalachian Reckoning: A Region Responds to Hillbilly Elegy*, ed. Anthony Harkins and Meredith McCarroll (Morgantown: West Virginia University Press, 2019), 278–89.

5   Ibid.; Paul Thompson and Richard and Joanna Bornat, *The Voice of the Past: Oral History* (Oxford: Oxford University Press, 2017).

6   Historians and anthropologists continue to be intrigued by the question of human historical agency, particularly with regard to marginalized and subaltern groups in national, transnational, and imperial settings. While postcolonial narratives of resistance (violent and nonviolent) continue to be useful for framing such studies, further questions related to the inclusion of voices of marginalized groups are constantly being debated by scholars. Beset by the biases, silences, and narrative limitations of the colonial and national archives, a number of historians of imperialism and colonialism have developed methods for reading such archives "against the grain," resuscitating the agency of marginalized and subaltern groups. However, when the historical subjects involved belong to nonliterate or primarily oral cultures, different approaches must be taken. In these cases, historians must rely on the data provided by alternative historical sources, such as archaeology, historical linguistics, and oral/life histories collected from historical subjects. John Edward Phillips, *Writing African History* (Rochester, NY: University of Rochester Press, 2005)

7   Portelli, *Oral History*, 21–30.

8   Karshner uses Rodger Cunningham's definition of *cosmovision*: "a systematic structure of meaning applying order to the cosmos; in short, a folk ideology and at the same time, a specifically, spiritual phenomenon"; Rodger Cunningham, "The Green Side of Life: Appalachian Magic as a Site of Resistance," *Appalachian Heritage*, Spring 2010, 54–62.

9   Karshner, "These Stories Sustain Me", 278–89.

10   Ibid., 285.

11   Ibid.

12   See, e.g., Herbert C. Covey, *African-American Slave Medicine: Herbal and Non-Herbal Treatments* (Lanham: Lexington Books, 2008).

13   Matthew Sparks, "The 'Charm Doctors' of Leslie County: Oral Histories of Male Witches, Midwives, and Faith Healers in Leslie County, Kentucky 1878–1978," *Bulletin of the Transilvania University of Brașov—Special Issue Series IV: Philology and Cultural Studies*, vol. 12, 61, no. 2 (2019).

14   Mary Sizemore interviewed by Diane Lewis in Leslie County, Kentucky, February 18, 1979; Tena-Baker Dean interviewed by author in Leslie County, Kentucky, December 16, 2018.

15   Mallie Sizemore, interviewed by Diane Lewis, February 18, 1979, Frontier Nursing Service Oral History Project, Louie B. Nunn Center for Oral History, University of Kentucky Libraries.

16   Tena Baker Dean, interviewed by Matthew Sparks, December 16, 2018.

17   Mary Brewer, *Rugged Trail to Appalachia* (Viper, KY: Graphic Arts Press, 1978), 114.

18   Matt Gray, interviewed by Dale Deaton, July 21, 1978, Frontier Nursing Service Oral History Project, Louie B. Nunn Center for Oral History, University of Kentucky Libraries.

19   Ibid.; scientific names have been added where possible.

20   Paul B. Hamel and Mary Ulmer Chiltoskey, *Cherokee Plants and Their Uses: A 400 Year History* (Sylva, NC: Herald Publishing, 2002).

21   Matt Gray, interviewed by Dale Deaton, July 21, 1978, Frontier Nursing Service Oral History Project, Louie B. Nunn Center for Oral History, University of Kentucky Libraries; scientific names were verified in Hamel and Ulmer Chiltosky, *Cherokee Plants*.

22   Matthew Sparks, "The Unsettling of Appalachia: Identity, Activism, and Appalachian Consciousness in Conversation with S-Town," *Activist History Review*, June 22, 2017, accessed October 9, 2021, https://tinyurl.com/2ry3nvjz.

23   This project is still ongoing, and as of yet the interviews have not been published. I plan on publishing the interviews on completion of the project. Select redacted transcripts can be made available upon request.

24   Ivy, twenty-six, Viper, Kentucky, at Country Queers, ed. Rachel Garringer, October 9, 2013, unavailable October 9, 2021, https://countryqueers.com/2013/10/09/4-ivy-26-viper-kentucky.

25   Ibid.

ABOUT THE AUTHOR

Matthew Ryan Sparks is a third-year PhD student in Middle East Studies at Ben Gurion University of the Negev, in Beersheva, Israel. He received his MA in Global, International and Comparative History from Georgetown University, and two BA's in History and Religion and Philosophy from Catawba College. A lifelong storyteller, Matthew is a published author, oral historian, and professional editor with four years of experience working with various international publishers in copyediting, proofreading, indexing, translation, and transcription. His interests include the oral/life histories and folklore of nomadic and subaltern populations (especially ethnobotany) in his native Central Appalachia, as well as the Middle East and North Africa. He is the cofounder of Sparks & McNeill, where he works as an editor, consultant, and workshop organizer. When he gets a break from the grind, Matthew enjoys gardening, homebrewing (and other homesteading activities), hiking, jam sessions, exploring ancient cities, playing dominos, and conversing for hours on end in stimulating settings. You can reach Matthew at: mrs290@georgetown.edu.

The Man, the Moth, the Legend: The Role and Function of Folklore in Queer-Appalachian Social Media Communities

Brent Watts

Introduction

The legend of the Mothman begins with a death. Someone had died, so there was need for a grave. So on the evening of November 12, 1966, five men set to digging in a cemetery near Clendenin, West Virginia. I'm sure they were used to this kind of work—they had done it dozens of times, and they thought this time would be no different. To these five men, I imagine gravedigging had become mundane. Maybe it was weird at first, but after the first few times it was just another job. There was probably a gentle breeze that day, and the rustling of the leaves allowed the creature to alight atop the trees without being heard. None of the men took notice as it watched them dig. If they heard or saw anything, they didn't think it was out of the ordinary. One thing is for sure: when the creature leaped from its perch and swooped down over the men's heads, they took notice. When they saw its human shape and massive wings, they knew that what they saw was more than just the wind.

Likewise, it was not the wind that haunted the "TNT area" just north of Point Pleasant, West Virginia, although it was reported to be just as fast. Once the site of a manufacturing plant and government storage facility for explosive materials, the TNT area is a forested eight thousand acres populated by a number of now abandoned earthen bunkers designed to minimize the level of destruction should their contents decide to explode. Some say the creature hoped to avoid humans and decided to call the TNT area its home. Whether or not this is true, that's certainly where the creature was when two teenage couples came upon it devouring a German Shepherd on the side of the road while out for a drive. Under the headlights of their car, they saw it: a "large flying man with ten-foot wings," whose eyes "glowed red."[1] Through its stoplight-red eyes, it saw them as well. Easily matching the top of speed of the car, it took flight as it pursued the vehicle through the TNT area. Somehow the teenagers managed to escape, but over the course of the next thirteen months more people reported similar experiences. Some, they say, were infected with a rare form of conjunctivitis (pink eye), caused by the creature's glowing red eyes. Others reported strange electrical phenomena, mysterious phone calls, and visits from men in black. Then, on December 15, 1967, tragedy struck. The Silver Bridge, which connected Point Pleasant, West Virginia, to Gallipolis, Ohio, collapsed, sending forty-six people to their deaths.[2] While experts reported it was due to a preventable architectural failure, many debated the cause. Some said it was just a failure, plain and simple. However, eyewitnesses reported seeing a strange, winged figure hunched atop one of the bridge towers and placed their blame accordingly. Still, others thought that the creature's relationship to the tragedy wasn't as the cause but, rather, as a harbinger sent to caution against, or even prevent, such a tragic loss of life.

After the collapse of the Silver Bridge, sightings of the Mothman in the area came to a halt. However, online forums still speak of the creature's reappearance in Chernobyl prior to the infamous nuclear disaster in 1986 and again in Moscow prior to the 1999 apartment bombings.[3] More recently, multiple sightings of the creature were reported in Chicago and around Lake Michigan throughout 2017 and were attributed by many to the turmoil of the 2016 presidential election and the subsequent inauguration of Donald Trump as president.[4] In 1975, John Keel published his book *The Mothman Prophecies*, and a 2002 film adaptation familiarized many people with the legend for the first time. Mothmen have also appeared as important characters in podcasts like *The Adventure Zone* by West Virginia's McElroy brothers and videogames like Bethesda's *Fallout 76* and Atlus's *Persona 5*. In addition to an ever-growing assortment of Mothman-themed food, drink, and memorabilia available in town and online, Point Pleasant today is also home to "The World's Only Mothman Museum." The museum collects and displays original artifacts and eyewitness accounts from each incident, including the Silver Bridge collapse, as well as props, wardrobe, and other paraphernalia from *The Mothman Prophecies* film. On the third weekend of every September, Point Pleasant hosts its annual Mothman Festival, a town-wide event, which features live music, cosplay contests, a five-kilometer run, and guest

speakers, such as original Mothman witnesses and noted cryptozoolo-
gists. The festival attracts over ten thousand people from the world over,
demonstrating how prominent the Mothman legend has become within
the cultural zeitgeist—even on a global scale.[5]

The prominence of the Mothman legend is for good reason. As
I demonstrate in this chapter, folklore is important to social interaction and meaning-making. The ways in which we talk about and engage
with folklore play a part in how we forge and express our identities
through interaction with others. Specifically, I show that talk about the
Mothman (and some other folkloric figures) serves a variety of purposes
in the online social media communities of queer-Appalachians. The most
notable of these purposes are 1) the reconciliation and union of queer
and Appalachian identities and 2) advocacy for leftist praxis and ideologies. These findings reveal how queer-Appalachians are (re)defining for
themselves what it means to be both queer and Appalachian, a (re)defini-
tion that flies in the face of all hegemonic descriptions of queerness and
Appalachia. I attribute this phenomenon, in part, to an attempt at reclaiming abusive rhetoric that describes both queer people and Appalachian (or
rural) people as dangerous "Others" who exist at the margins of societies
and pose a threat to the majority. In other words, by aligning themselves
with these conceptual figures to which maligners may readily compare
them, queer (and) Appalachian people are able to, in a sense, disarm the
abusive rhetoric and mitigate potential emotional or social harm.

Methods and Positionality

I view language as a form of social practice, a notion that positions
discourse as a robust substrate for the identification and examination
of power relations and social inequities.[6] This position also means that
I view language and social practices as mutually constitutive—that
language and social practices cyclically and continuously justify and
produce one another. Drawing from complexity theory, I also view
language as a complex, adaptive system; an ongoing process that is
capable of changing or stabilizing in response to the sociocultural environment.[7] This is an important distinction for the research at hand, in
that it allows me to talk about queer-Appalachian Mothman discourse
as an adaptation to the social context. This is to say that in a discourse
context that complicates queer-Appalachian identity work through
homophobia and rural heteronormativity the language system will evolve

to suit the social needs of its users. Furthermore, I believe that any structures or patterns we might perceive in the system, best described here perhaps as "queer-Appalachianness," are emergent. This caveat prevents the overgeneralization of things like discursive practices, such as talk about Mothman, to groups who don't necessarily use them and centers the fact that communication through language is a process through which identity, as most conceptualize it, is produced.

Lastly, there are some other important concepts necessary for any discourse analytic approach. First are *signs*, which, like the name might imply, are things that mean something else. The three kinds of signs are *icons*, *symbols*, and *indexes*. An *icon* refers to its referent through resemblance or representation. For example, gendered restrooms might communicate their "genderedness" through the use of signs with simple graphic representations of "men" (🚹) and "women" (🚺). Likewise, *symbol* is used to describe the kind of sign that refers to its referent through an arbitrary relationship. Again, gendered restrooms may communicate their genderedness through the Mars (♂) and Venus (♀) symbols, which have arbitrarily come to refer to "maleness" and "femaleness," respectively. Lastly, there are *indexes*. Indexes communicate their meaning by indirectly "pointing" to a referent that is tied to context. An indexical take on the gendered restroom example might feature a man's shoe (👞) on the men's room door and a high-heel shoe (👠) on the women's room door. In this example, these indexical signs convey "maleness" and "femaleness" through a shared context in which men (are expected to) wear flat-heel shoes and women (are expected to) wear high-heel shoes. Because of a shared context, these indexes are successful signs, but in a culture where this context doesn't exist, they simply could not work.

In addition to appearing as graphical representations, icons, symbols, and indexes also appear throughout every human language system. For example, language-based icons usually take the form of onomatopoeia, which sonically resemble the things they refer to; these include words like *achoo* and *meow* but also words like *drip*, *sizzle*, and *splash*. Conversely, most words are *symbolic*; the relationship between the word and its meaning is purely arbitrary. For example, there is nothing about the word *dog*, either written or spoken, that looks or sounds like a dog. Therefore, *dog* means *a canine pet*, because everyone who uses the word to mean that agrees that it does. Language-based indexes, or indexical signs, are the primary site of analysis for the research I present here. Now, y'all might best understand indexical signs by thinking about this very sentence. Certainly, it's clear that I am addressing you, the audience, by saying *y'all*. However, by saying *y'all*, a lot more is also being communicated, or, more specifically, *indexed*. My use of *y'all* likely indexes something about being (and/or wanting to be seen as) country, rural, Southern, or something similar. It might also index a level of informality that you weren't expecting based on past experiences you've had with texts of this nature. Because of the context, it might even index something about the author's disregard for prescriptive writing standards. The variability of indexical meaning is especially integral to discourse analysis, because it allows for the communication and proliferation of socially important, nonliteral meaning, in addition, of course, to its literal meaning.

The continuous process through which signs are used to produce contexts and contexts are used to produce signs is mutually constitutive—the existence of one affords and justifies the other. Though a circular interpretation of this process seems intuitive, it is also helpful to conceive of this process as sedimentary in nature. In other words, each time a sign is successfully used to establish a particular context, as well as each time a sign conveys a particular meaning against a particular context, a new precedent is created. Layer by layer, new possibilities for communication are made possible. For this project, the most important version of this process is called "enregisterment," the process through which linguistic forms become linked to (or indexical of) social meaning.[8] Enregisterment describes three different levels of indexical "awareness." First-order indexical signs can be correlated with social meaning, although to those who use them, they are likely not noticeable, because "everybody speaks that way." Second-order indexical signs are more noticeable and are available for social work, meaning people can use and manipulate them to create social meaning for themselves and others. Third-order indexical signs are more highly noticeable and often comprise some of the most stereotyped linguistic forms; these kinds of indexical signs essentialize linguistic form to social meaning (i.e., every way of being has a related way of speaking). In this research, I make the somewhat novel argument that certain discursive subjects, such as the Mothman legend, can become enregistered just like dialectal features or words, such that when someone talks about the Mothman legend in the right context, they may be indexing the fact that they are queer and/or Appalachian, whether or not they themselves are aware of doing it.

Contextualizing the Mothman

The Mothman belongs to a group known as "cryptids," a distinction it shares with other folkloric figures such as Bigfoot, El Chupacabra, and the Loch Ness Monster. Cryptids are creatures whose existence is assumed by believers or followers of the pseudoscience known as cryptozoology. Note that the term "pseudoscience" in this context is used to distinguish this way of thought from more rigorous scientific methodologies. In the interest of constructing a fair depiction of folkloric discourse, I do not intend to suggest that witnesses or believers in the Mothman and associated phenomena are in any way categorically lacking in character or credibility.[9] Instead, it must be acknowledged that cryptozoology, like other scientifically unsubstantiated belief systems, is based on the faith and practices of the community that upholds it. As far as I am concerned, the issue is not so much whether or not the creature is real but, rather, what people are doing by engaging in talk about the creature and its legendry.

I am more so interested in the acknowledgment of nontraditional takes on the Mothman legend and its subsequent incorporation into mainstream study and interest. This task is of great importance, as the legend takes on a more globalized and mass media–mediated nature, becoming less folkloric and more media-loric. This means that a cultural figure, regardless of whether it has roots in traditional community-based folklore or in popular culture, underwent substantial characterization and development from popular media, such that part of its character in the public imagination is attributable to popular media. A good example of such a legend is that of the mermaid, whose many and varied portrayals in books and movies and on television throughout history have established it more as a fixture of popular imagery and less as a feature of any one specific group.

In writing about the Tanzanian Popobawa, a legendary creature similar to the Mothman, Katrina Daly Thompson, professor and chair of African Cultural Studies at the University of Wisconsin–Madison, expounds upon the ways in which people talk about the Popobawa in order to "do" queer identity work. She argues that there is actually much at stake as the Popobawa begins to go global, spreading from Tanzania and moving "beyond the boundaries of its culture of origin . . . [able to] be repurposed."[10] Given the Mothman's continued prominence in the global public imagination and its more recent inclusion in popular media, the Mothman legend's potential for globalization may also allow for the diffusion and spread of other meanings associated with talk about the legend; namely, in this case, queerness, Appalachianness, and queer-Appalachianness. Thinking back to mermaids, we might question what features of the legend have survived as the figures have become increasingly mediated by popular culture, as well as which features have been subverted or otherwise changed since their more "traditional" inceptions. Examples of similar phenomena, wherein linguistic or discursive features are expressly associated with culturally or socially salient icons and practices through the medium of videogames, can be found in previous literature.[11]

Analysis: Mothman as Queer-Appalachian

The data under analysis was collected from the Instagram account of the Queer Appalachia Project, @queerappalachia. According to their official website, Queer Appalachia is a memorial project for the late Bryn Kelly, a trans woman writer, artist, activist, and self-proclaimed "Granny Witch."[12] The Queer Appalachia Instagram account began in 2016 to create an online community and resource collective for queer-Appalachians and Southerners.[13] Broadly, the project focuses on reclaiming and redefining queer (and) Appalachian narratives, as well as fostering mutual aid and harm reduction efforts, especially as they relate to the opioid crisis and other public health issues currently afflicting Appalachia and the South.[14] In the course of this analysis, I present three categories of Mothman-centric Instagram posts made by Queer Appalachia: Mothman as queer-Appalachian, Mothman as Appalachian, and Mothman as queer. This order was chosen to demonstrate the parallel and mutually constitutive processes that have allowed for interpretations of Mothman as each of the categories and, I believe, the real-time enregisterment of "Mothman talk" as indexical of queer-Appalachian. That said, the first post to be considered contains the image presented in figure 1.

Figure 1 depicts a (rather muscular) paper doll Mothman with colorful wings, photoshopped into the foreground of a picture of an actual field. The background features what looks like the rolling green hills of the Appalachian Mountains. The accompanying comment from Queer Appalachia (QA) is " #jortseason is cum'n & #blueridgemountain #mothman is feel'n it! #showusyoutjortscollaboration." He wears denim cutoff shorts (jorts), a plaid bowtie, and nothing else. Alone, each of these facts may seem rather insignificant. However, taken in conjunction with

Figure 1: "Jort Season is Cum'n 4/21" (Queer Appalachia 2019b)

the context shared between the author and the imagined audience (i.e., Queer Appalachia and queer-Appalachians), these facts constitute a larger discourse about ruralness, queerness, Appalachia(ns), and the Mothman that, to the uninformed viewer, is not as informative, but, to the informed viewer, is immensely informative. Take, for example, the Blue Ridge Mountain wings; should they miss the #blueridgemoutain hashtag, the average Instagram user may only register the wings as a gradient of color, not a mountain range. However, a user with the shared context assumed by QA, taking into consideration the other facts about the picture, is likely to know that the wings depict the Blue Ridge Mountains. Furthermore, the user whose shared context includes the cultural and geographical importance of the Blue Ridge Mountains to Appalachia can interpret the wings' design as an indexical sign that points to *Appalachia(n)*, and *rural*, among other potential meanings. This indexical relationship is strengthened by the indexical signs of the overgrown field and the mountains in the background, which point toward *ruralness*, and, in turn, *Appalachia(n)*, due to its rural associations. The indexical relationship between this image and *Appalachia(n)* is strengthened even further by Mothman's attire. For one, the jorts call to mind the image of Daisy Duke from TV's *The*

Dukes of Hazzard and the original poster girl for denim cutoffs. Through indexical association with *The Dukes of Hazzard*, the meanings of *rural* and *Southern* are also communicated. Likewise, the plaid pattern on the bowtie evokes the image of country and western wear and points toward *Southernness, ruralness,* and *country-ness.* However, both the jorts and the bowtie also index, both directly and indirectly, *queerness.* After all, Mothman is, presumably, a man. His drawn anatomy (no doubt modeled after the equally muscular statue in Point Pleasant) also seems to confirm this. Therefore, this places Mothman in the realm of gendered things. In conjunction with his six-pack abs, the bowtie and jorts make Mothman look like a male stripper, therefore indirectly indexing something about *intense or overt sexuality.* This indexical meaning is reinforced by the respelling of *coming* as *cum'n.* In this light, the fact that Mothman is wearing Daisy Dukes also seems to suggest a subversion of cishetero-normative assumptions about gender, sexuality, and gender expression. Furthermore, the queer reinterpretation of the Daisy Dukes, given the associations attached to their show of origin, and in the context of the QA account itself, is also likely to index something about disassociation from and opposition to white supremacy, the Confederacy, and anti-Black ideologies. Should this indexical meaning be successfully conveyed, it is of special interest, because it represents one of many examples of QA and their audience reimagining Appalachia and the South as a place of queerness, Blackness, and antifascist action.

Created by Appalachian cartoonist Bryan Richards (Instagram: @best.virginia) as a submission for *Dinner Bell* magazine and reposted by QA, figure 2 depicts a chubby and cartoonish Mothman sitting on a billboard overlooking a highway. The billboard depicts the logo of the popular restaurant franchise, Tudor's Biscuit World. As Mothman chews on a biscuit, a vehicle on the highway below emits a heart. In this example, Tudor's Biscuit World, Mothman, and a potential Appalachian (the driver) are semiotically juxtaposed to one another. This post is of note in that it represents one layer of the sedimentary process that has allowed for the (re)interpretation of Mothman as *Appalachian.* For one, it clearly features Tudor's at center, which is a well-known and much-loved Central Appalachian institution. Given that a sign for Tudor's is only likely to be in or near Appalachia, it can be assumed that the setting for this picture is Appalachia, and the driver of the vehicle below is also Appalachian. Regardless, it is certain that the centering of Tudor's in this artwork

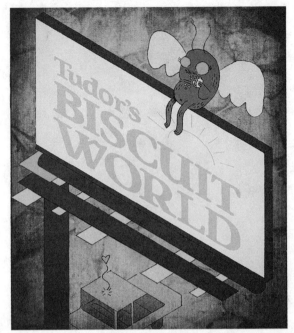

Figure 2: Mothman and Tudor's Biscuit World (Queer Appalachia 2019a)

is intended to index *Appalachia(n)*, if not also *familiarity for* or even *love for Appalachia*. Keeping with this line of logic, it would then follow that Mothman is, if anything, Appalachian as well; if not, it would seem that he at least likes Appalachian food. If the heart emitted by the driver is intended for Mothman, then it would seem that Mothman also has the approval of an Appalachian. All these facts seem to point toward a set of similar indexical meanings: Mothman, Appalachia, and Tudor's all somehow belong or fit together.

The image in figure 3 again depicts the paper doll Mothman, but with colorful wings reminiscent of the Pride flag. Cosplaying as Dr. Frank-N-Furter from the cult classic *Rocky Horror Picture Show*, he wears glittery black lingerie and a pearl necklace. The indexical meaning of *queer*, and by extension the indexical characterization of Mothman as an overtly sexual queer man, is clearly expressed in this image and the accompanying text, in much the same way it was in figure 1. Additionally, by invoking the text of *Rocky Horror Picture Show* and other texts related to the film, QA is also pointing toward the camp style and sensibilities that have long been associated with queer art and culture. The creature stands in front of what looks like a red velvet curtain, calling to mind the theater space

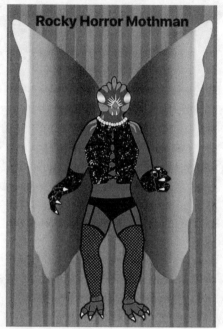

Figure 3: Rocky Horror Mothman (Queer Appalachia 2018a; 2018b)

seen at the end of the film, as well as the drama and glamour stereotypi-
cally associated with theater spaces and queer people in theater spaces,
a move that, in this case, could be seen as an act of reclamation of potentially homophobic tropes. In this instance, viewers see the Mothman as
someone who is distinctly queer, and it is only through the Appalachian
context of the account and accompanying post that one can further link
Mothman, in this instance, with Appalachianness and in turn, queer-
Appalachianness. The post's text is as follows:

> #rockyhorror#mothman w/ #blueridgemountainwings 8x10 print
> $9.99 ALL profits buy winter coats for rural queers in need in the
> region. If you need a winter coat, email us through our website, both
> links in bio. If you're one of the folks that we have already helped
> get ready for winter this month, please consider writing us a note
> through our website that we can share with our followers.[15]

Again, QA outright links Mothman to the Blue Ridge Mountains and,
by extension, Appalachia. Furthermore, in this instance, Mothman is
used as a rallying symbol for coat donations to other "rural queers in
need in the region." In addition to depicting Mothman as queer, this

post directly links Mothman as a figure to the well-being of those in the Appalachian region, and especially those in the Appalachian region who are also queer and/or in need. Furthermore, by not visually depicting the Mothman in this instance as distinctly Appalachian, Queer Appalachia may indirectly be suggesting that queerness is queerness, no matter where it is. Alternatively, they may be suggesting that Mothman is an Appalachian enough symbol that dressing him as Frank-N-Furter gets the "queer-Appalachian" point across in a sufficiently succinct way, without any additions necessary. Importantly, this post also represents one of the most common kinds of posts on QA's Instagram: those about mutual aid and harm reduction. Although this instance is more atypical of that type of post, it nonetheless is representative of both QA's distinct leftist (re) imagining of Appalachia, as well as the association of Mothman with a distinct brand of leftist theory and praxis that is uniquely colored by the lived experiences of queer-Appalachians.

Conclusion

This research demonstrates that folkloric discourse is rife with oppor-tunities for meaning-making and identity work. In this case, Mothman discourse can at least be used for identity work related to Appalachian, queer, and queer-Appalachian identities. In engaging with Mothman discourse in this way, queer (and) Appalachian people can assert them-selves as different from normative society, due to either their queer and/ or Appalachian status. Furthermore, for language users who are both queer *and* Appalachian, engagement with and use of Mothman discourse and iconography can allow them a safe ideological space in which they can manage and maintain two nonnormative identities whose coexist-ence is discouraged or obscured by more normative ideologies. In doing so, they forge a much needed way forward for queer-Appalachian ways of talking and being. Additionally, through Mothman discourse, members of this community can also reimagine and redefine Appalachia in ways that challenge mainstream narratives about the region. In doing so, the QA community is able to present a different kind of Appalachia, one that has long been obscured by dominant narratives, one that centers mutual aid, harm reduction, and antifascist resistance and allows for the reconciliation of queer-Appalachian and other seemingly at odds identi-ties. These findings represent what I believe to be a truth about folklore: insofar as we create and tell stories, so too do we create the mental and social space necessary for those stories to exist. In fact, the imaginative breadth of folklore makes it especially well-situated for transgressive and innovative social meaning-making and identity work. It affords new possibilities for being and interacting, and, in doing so, creates the potential to make imaginary futures real, even if the stories that got us there might not be.

NOTES

1   Joe Nickell, *The Mystery Chronicles: More Real-Life X-Files* (Lexington: University of Kentucky Press, 2004), 93–99.

2   Chris LeRose, "The Collapse of the Silver Bridge," *West Virginia Historical Society Quarterly* 15, no. 4 (2001).

3   Denis Lobkov, "Призраки катастроф", *Zheltaya Gazeta via Svobodnaya Gruziya*, May 23, 2002, 6.

4   Tobias Wayland, *The Lake Michigan Mothman: High Strangeness in the Midwest* (self-published, 2019).

5   Erin (Perkins) Johnson, "Mothman Festival Returns Sept. 21–22", *Point Pleasant Register*, September 6, 2019, accessed October 9, 2021, https://www.mydailyregister.com/news/44780/mothman-festival-returns-sept-21-22.

6   As a linguistic anthropologist, the framework and theory with which I operate necessitate an interdisciplinary component. Therefore, the methodology used in this project is best described as a multimodal critical discourse analysis (MMCDA), an approach grounded in both linguistic theory and critical theory.

7   For example, Podesva and Van Hofwegen found the pronunciation of /s/ among speakers in small-town California varied regularly according to social dimensions such as gender identity, gender expression, sexuality, and rural-urban alignment; Robert Podesva and Janneke Van Hofwegen, "/s/exuality in Smalltown California: Gender Normativity and the Acoustic Realization of /s/," in *Language, Sexuality, and Power: Studies in Intersectional Sociolinguistics*, eds. Ezra Levon and Ronald Beline Mendes (Oxford: Oxford University Press, 2015), 168–88.

8   Barbara Johnstone, Jennifer Andrus, and Andrew E. Danielson, "Mobility, Indexicality, and the Enregisterment of 'Pittsburghese,'" *Journal of English Linguistics* 34, no. 2, (June 2006).

9   Katrina Daly Thompson, *Popobawa: Tanzanian Talk, Global Misreadings* (Bloomington: Indiana University Press, 2017).

10   Ibid., 101.

11   For example, Mendoza-Denton found that creaky voice (or "vocal fry") in certain communities of practice, had become associated with a "hardcore Chicana/o" persona, and that this marker had been picked up and amplified by Rockstar's 2004 *Grand Theft Auto: San Andreas* in the interest of representing a Chicano gangster character; Norma Mendoza-Denton, "The Semiotic Hitchhiker's Guide to Creaky Voice: Circulation and Gendered Hardcore in a Chicana/o Gang Persona," *Linguistic Anthropology* 21, no. 2 (December 2011): 261–80.

12   Queer Appalachia, "Femmespiration," accessed November 9, 2021, https://tinyurl.com/yww93ywm.

13   Samantha Manzella, *Meet the Queer-Appalachians Using Social Media to Cultivate Community in the Rural South*, NewNowNext, 2018, accessed November 9, 2021, https://tinyurl.com/8nfty8em.

14   For the purposes of this chapter, I solely considered posts about Mothman that are emblematic of a few of the categories identified in my master's thesis (forthcoming). There are other categories featuring other folkloric figures and figures from popular culture, but for brevity's sake I have omitted them.

15   Queer Appalachia, @jacobtobia made a thoughtful moth series earlier in the week. It was missing my favorite #westvirginiamoth #queerappalachia #electricdirt #mothman (ed.) @queerappalachia: Instagram, 2018a.

ABOUT THE AUTHOR

Brent Watts is a first-generation college student from Breathitt County, in Eastern Kentucky. He graduated from the University of Kentucky in May 2018 with dual BAs in International Studies and Theatre and minors in Spanish and Linguistics. He is a recent graduate from the MA in Linguistic Theory and Typology program at the University of Kentucky. There, he developed an interest in linguistic anthropological methods as a means for researching and advocating for queer (and) Appalachian ways of life. In his work as a playwright and arts educator, queer Appalachia usually takes center stage once again. He hopes to be able to use his research in tandem with his art to advocate for Appalachia and its people, as well as to establish meaningful connections and build intergroup solidarity between Appalachians and groups with similar experiences of marginalization.

Crafting Queer Histories of Technology

Hannah Conway

I had the distinct pleasure of copyediting most of the pieces for this project and getting to spend time with the work and words of each of my fellow contributors. What has emerged for me in this reading is a theme of identity-making: of finding ways to yourself and to your work in places and spaces where personal identities don't sit easy with one another or have been violently omitted from the dominant narrative, and then navigating what kind of obligations those identities give us to ourselves, to each other, to the places we're from and maybe left or that we still call home. Even in the pieces that focus on activism, identity is central, if not explicit. Folks fight for the places or people they feel connected to, that they share in an identity-making (or remaking) project with, or that they have always called home but have been denied full participation in because of race, gender, or sexual identity. For queer Appalachians, that almost always means fighting against parts of the standard identity, one that is steeped in white supremacy, settler colonialism, distrust and hatred of those things that are "queer." In thinking through my own contribution to this archive of queer Appalachia, I have felt similarly compelled to use this space to grapple with identity, how it informs my work when I walk into an archive or a field site or sit down to write and why I think it's important that we undertake these identity-making and archiving projects with care.

Like many Appalachian writers before me, I did not have a sense of an "Appalachian" identity before I moved out of the South. Despite growing up in rural southwest Virginia, just outside of Roanoke, and even attending Appalachian State University. I didn't think of Appalachia as a distinct region or of myself as distinct because of my upbringing there until I moved to the vastly different cultural world of Cambridge, Massachusetts, in the summer of 2015. This identity was heightened following the 2016 election, when Appalachia was quickly painted as a scapegoat, the heart of "Trump country," the source of a creeping tide of backwardness, hate, and bigotry. As a historian and progressive with roots in Southern Appalachia, suddenly facing the barrage of stereotypical insults about my home, I rushed to find ways to defend the place that I was from despite all of its complications and darkness. It wasn't that these stereotypes were new to me, but they felt different when they came from the mouths of New England academics armed only with flattened understandings of the region and its complexities. This displacement of blame also seemed disingenuous, just one short bridge over from Boston—one of the whitest and most notoriously racist cities in the country—which sits well beyond the Appalachians and above the Mason-Dixon line.[1]

The thing is that I never felt like I fit in where I grew up either. My parents aren't from the small mountain town they raised me in, and we didn't have the same deep familial connections there as many people in the county. They're also politically progressive and atheist, which has always set our family apart from the community. While both of these things made me feel ostracized when I was a child, as a punk teenager during the rise of post-9/11 nationalism and the reign of Bush II, I took pride in our nonconformity and couldn't wait to get out of my hometown and never look back. It wasn't until I was in my twenties and could visit with some distance from growing up there that I came to appreciate Appalachia as the place that raised me, and as a unique cultural region with a rich history that was much deeper than the surface narrative that often represents it. But this feeling of a lack of Appalachian "roots" is increasingly complex for me. My father, grandmother, and I are citizens of the Cherokee Nation of Oklahoma, and the ancestral land our family was removed from in the 1870s was in what is now known as northern, Appalachian Georgia. While "Appalachia," as the area is currently organized and characterized, is a regional identity largely rooted in white settler culture, my distant kin were indigenous to the land it grew upon, and its development depended on their (and other tribal groups') violent erasure from the physical and cultural landscape. Appalachian land is doubly my home, so why do I feel a sense of inauthenticity when I try to claim it?

I also took my time finding my queer identity. Unlike many other queer-Appalachian authors, I never had a coming-out moment that I can pinpoint as a specific acknowledgment of my identity or that I navigated as an experience of trauma tied to choosing to be openly queer.[2] Rather, I have always just been "out" to my close friends, and I've only talked vaguely about my queerness with certain members of my family. My parents always made it known that they accepted me regardless of my identity, and I've used that blessing paired with a natural inclination to keep my personal life quite private to sidestep confronting it. It's only in the last few years that I've begun to unpack the ways I internalized the explicit and often violent homophobia and transphobia I grew up around socially and culturally and how it impacted my own acceptance of my identity as a queer person, as well as how it informed what I now understand is a reluctance to be fully out in many spaces.

Working through my personal identities and growing into my career as a historian are processes that have happened alongside one another—I couldn't recognize myself as Appalachian until I saw the erasure of people like me from the dominant narrative about the region, couldn't understand myself as being queer until I reckoned with what it meant to grow up queer in such a complicated place, didn't fully grasp how marginalized Indigenous scholarship and knowledge was until I had to seek it out after it was omitted from class after class. I didn't do any of these things until I was well into graduate school and began thinking about the craft of storytelling embedded in the study of history and how my identities impacted the kinds of stories I wanted to tell and the voices I sought to find in the archives and the field. I did not pursue history as an undergrad—my first degree is in photography—and when I began to study history I was interested in the early-modern sciences in Europe. But over time, my work became increasingly modern, and my interest in the linkages between technology and state power, particularly in the twentieth-century US South, came into focus. By my second year at Harvard and the first year of my PhD, I was working with my advisor on the history of environmental regulation and legislation in the mid- to late twentieth-century US, and I knew I wanted to continue to do work that informed and impacted the present as much as it told compelling stories about the past.

For me, doing that meant writing about places and peoples I cared about deeply from a place of positionality: a place of recognizing my own identity and its role in how I tell stories, what kinds of knowledges I seek to produce, what kinds of privileges that knowledge reflects, and the responsibility that comes along with claiming an identity personally and academically. I have spent a great deal of time while working toward completing my dissertation asking myself what exactly it means to be Appalachian, queer, and to hold tribal citizenship—and to acknowledge these as parts of myself and my scholarship—as a historian of science and technology. Each of these identities feels like it comes saddled both with the task of proving authenticity—Do you really belong here? Do your people claim you?[3]—and with the obligation to produce work that benefits the community. Can folks from academically marginalized groups produce scholarship simply for the sake of knowledge production, or is there an implicit expectation that we do something better than the extractive practices academia has so often built itself upon? Can we use community- or identity-informed methodologies of care to tell more layered and complex stories about the past in the hope of changing these troublesome narratives and building a better future?

Queering the History of Technology

It was with this jumble of thoughts about identity, storytelling, and the history of technology that I headed into the collections of the Tennessee Valley Authority (TVA) at the National Archives just outside of Atlanta the past two summers. My dissertation is about the realities that are created through infrastructure construction and aging—how the built world builds worlds and how they impact the worlds we live in now. I am particularly interested in how pieces of infrastructure become embedded in the environment, as well as in the social and cultural systems into which they are constructed, and in doing so, how they become systems of control. In many ways infrastructures, like other pieces of technology, are inherently normative structures.[4] Interrogating why they were built in certain places, at certain times, by certain people, beyond narratives of progress or necessity for technological advance, can tell complex stories about how dominant systems of power are reinforced in the built world around us.[5] I went to the archives to find documents related to the construction of the Allen Fossil Plant just south of Memphis, Tennessee, one of my dissertation field sites, but the story of Memphis is just one of thousands in the collection that illuminates how the TVA used large technological systems of infrastructure to remake the Appalachian and Deep South.[6]

The archives of the TVA are immense, holding over fourteen thousand cubic feet of records. During my time there, I've dug through technical plans, correspondences, legal cases, thousands of pages of inventories of materials and properties, maps of all kinds, various reports, publications, educational materials, and magazine and newspaper clippings. Most of these things I expected to find—but I was overwhelmed by the social scientific material the seemingly technical organization also produced that is housed there. The "Regional Studies and Surveys of the Social and Economic Division" subgroup of the collection is a patchwork quilt of data gathered from across the Tennessee Valley in the earliest years of the authority—almost all of the 390 folders appear to contain information compiled or generated between 1932 and 1934. These boxes include things like reports about: "isolated communities" undertaken by sociologists at the University of Tennessee; the impact on the education of rural students in Alabama in 1932 and 1933, when public school funding was so reduced that some counties cut their school years down to as little as forty-five days; a map identifying the location of homes and basic socioeconomic statistics of the family of every juvenile offender in the city I grew up just down the road from, Roanoke, Virginia, from 1924–1931.[7] In attempting to reconstruct the Tennessee Valley, the TVA was heavily invested in documenting a far-reaching archive about the region, its environment, and the people that lived there.

One piece of the collection that particularly caught my eye was the extensive series of photographs captured by New York photographer and sociologist Lewis Hine of the first town the TVA flooded, Loyston, Tennessee, and the detailed accompanying documentation of the removal of 2,900 people from the township.[8] The traditional story that the TVA told about itself and that was portrayed in publications and documentary-type films from the 1930s and 1940s painted a portrait of an Appalachian region in desperate need of salvation. Scenes typical of this particular kind of poverty porn often depicted an overworked, barren environment hopelessly tended by farmers with rudimentary equipment, skinny livestock, and run-down dogtrot farmhouses, their porches crowded with indigent elderly family members and too many barefoot children. A dichotomy was presented of stagnation and progress: Appalachia was portrayed as a region stuck firmly in the past, and the TVA positioned as a morally and technologically ambitious project that would combine the power of planning and ingenuity to allow farmers to pull themselves up by their bootstraps and rapidly move the region toward a new, modern, productive future. The only way for Appalachians out of poverty and destitution was the TVA and its technological salvation.

But the Hine photographs show a different picture of Appalachia, if you view them as portraits of lifeways removed from commodity and industrial capitalism, rather than as examples of an imposed narrative of intolerably hard living. In his work, he captured families going about their daily lives on their farms and in their houses in the rhythms of predominantly subsistence rural living: producing sorghum syrup, spinning textiles, or gathered together around the hearth at the end of the day in houses they had built by hand—most of the homes in the images are modest but tidy and well-kept—as well as some of larger modern-looking farmhouses, of churchgoers lined up before Sunday services with their black cars parked in a line along the dirt road, and of engaged children in a one-room schoolhouse ready to learn. These snapshots of Loyston come together to show the viewer a small but vibrant rural community, not a hopeless wasteland. I'm not trying to romanticize poverty or negate the fact that economic stagnation was (and still is) a very real and harmful concern for many Appalachian families. But the narrative of overwhelming Appalachian destitution isn't found in these images unless you equate all subsistence living with "poor" living. Hine also focused his camera on individual citizens and captured intimate details of the faces of the town, not only with his film but also with his notes. On the back of one photograph from a series of compelling portraits of a local man, he inscribed:

> "I love my mountains, an' I want to stay right here all the rest of my life if I can."
> —Curtis Stiner, a high grade mountain farmer, belongs to the Stiners of Union County—has lived here all his life and now the flood area will take his home. Now he has a job as "Sawyer" on the Dam Site. He is as picturesque in spirit and as sincere, as the photo-study shows him.[9]

The project of the TVA in Appalachian memory has also taken on a different character than the story of "democracy on the march" against wasteful misuse of the region that the Authority and its champions sought to tell about themselves. Many of the folks impacted by TVA displacement emphasize the period of rapid dam construction as one of trauma and loss for thousands of Appalachian families.[10] Elizabeth Catte, Appalachian Studies scholar and descendent of a family removed from Loyston, discussed the conflicted feelings her family had about their displacement in her 2018 book *What You Are Getting Wrong about Appalachia*.[11] Southern literary magazine the *Bitter Southerner* has also featured a number of excellent examinations of the impact of the TVA on Appalachian communities, including the recent photo essay "Dangerous Waters," by North Carolina–based photographer Micah Cash.[12] TVA floods have been immortalized by musicians, in films, and in stories about the restless ghosts the Authority roused when it inundated houses, towns, and graves with dam floodwaters.[13] In addition to these shared cultural critiques, continued concerns over extensive coal ash pollution from TVA power plants, amplified after the massive Kingston, Tennessee, spill in 2008, have tarnished the Authority's public reputation in recent years. But the Hine photographs and records from the removal of Loyston town folks show that the relationship between the TVA and the people it meant to serve has never been an easy one.[14]

In the 2020 collection *Storytelling in Queer Appalachia*, author and activist Adam Denney knits creative narrative and oral history together to draw connections between the TVA flood from the construction of the Wolf Creek Dam in Russell County, Kentucky, and experiences of growing up queer in Appalachia. In his story "A Drowning in the Foothills," he writes, "The aquatic simulacrums of the river bottoms I imagined as a child—the decomposing churches, cemeteries, farms, and schoolhouses—are more than necromantic renderings curated by an impressionable mind. They have provided a unique way for me to express and understand my experience of growing up as a rural queer in the Bible Belt." Denney reminds us that there are many different ways to drown in a place like Appalachia, and that queer folk in the region are "experts at holding our breath."[15] There are few queer ancestors to be explicitly found in the archives of the TVA—although they were also inarguably flooded off their land. Historical queer kin have always and will always live in Appalachia, even if they aren't named or didn't have the means or language to name themselves in our archives. But, like Denney, I have found the connections between the TVA and Appalachian queerness to be generative to think with and to tell stories through.

In my work, I flip the metaphor around and think about how queerness and queer theories can explain certain phenomena encountered in the archive. As I looked through the images captured by Hine, I wondered why the persistent narrative of Appalachia perpetuated in writing about the TVA painted these folks as backward, primitive, or unmodern. Their lives were as present and as modern as the TVA engineers that built the dams that took their homes from them; something else was at play that denied them full access to the present by relegating them to the past. What I found in these pictures was a queer sense of time, a representation of "queer time" as expressed by Jack Halberstam to be time frames occupied by those that threaten, or do not fit neatly within, normative ways of life.[16] In its rendering as a place sitting stagnant in the past, in which "modernity" is a goal to achieve not a point on a timeline, Appalachia has been discursively queered for the greater part of the twentieth century. It has been suspended in a never-where of the past and denied access to the present as long as it remained an unruly and "unproductive" part of the body of the nation-state. Rather than being seen as a viable alternative, another proposed future where the TVA and Appalachians worked together to mold the region without extensive displacement and dispossession, Appalachian resistance to the TVA was framed as the denial of any Appalachian future, a disregard for the normal patterns of intergenerational (re)productivity, an unacceptable answer to a demand that was never a question.

Bringing queer theory to bear on both Appalachian Studies and the history of technology illuminates how the people and the land of the region have been viewed as removed from the logics of rational capitalist production and time scales. TVA reformers focused on Appalachia's future possibilities for reform through technological salvation, while failing to actually disrupt the systems of settler colonialism, white supremacy, and extraction capitalism that undergird social, cultural, and economic stagnation in the region. While the TVA turned the lights on in the Appalachian South, the "modernity" it insisted the region needed to save itself was never fully realized as promised. Narratives of backwardness and irrevocable economic and moral poverty continued throughout the middle of the twentieth century, became a focal point of social crusaders in the 1960s and 1970s after president LBJ declared the "War on Poverty" while touring through Central Appalachia and signed the Appalachian Regional Development Act in 1965, and once again came to the fore after the 2016 election.

Because of the explicit elaboration of queer time by postcolonial scholars and literatures, viewing the Appalachian archives of the TVA with queer time frames also connects this moment to other colonized places and bodies. Doing so reminds us that while the stories of loss that come out of the TVA floods are compelling and representative of deeply felt community and personal loss, this history is more complicated. While not every family removed by the TVA was white by any means, Black Appalachians also lost their land and homes to the TVA, every white Appalachian claim to land was a settler claim.[17] This land is twice stolen and people who called this area home twice dispossessed, with pipeline companies currently working hard on a third dispossession. White Appalachians that stood in defense of their land claims against the TVA did so because of the eradication of Cherokee, Chickasaw, Muskogee, Catawba, Moneton, and other peoples from the land. Appalachia, like much of the United States, is a doubly colonized space; the connections between the dispossession of Indigenous peoples and dispossession of Appalachian settlers through a hierarchy of white, capitalist-industrial entitlement to land are something that historians of infrastructure and technology in the region continually need to reckon with when we go into the archive and sit down to write our histories, if we want to tell them thorough and compelling stories about the past.

Layering the Appalachian Landscape

There are always many ways to tell a story, to tell a history. The TVA "march of democracy narrative" is representative of one way: a flattened imaginary that simplifies a complex landscape. But to fully understand the history of this technological development we have to reconstitute the fullness of the story through the archive, through visual and cultural ethno-historiographic depictions, through the collective remembering of Appalachian folk—particularly those most marginalized in traditional histories. The history of infrastructure is never just the history of concrete and metal and wires. It is always also the history of the people and places bound up in those webs and of the other possible futures that existed before these large technological systems swallowed them up and foreclosed them.

Landscapes are multilayered things—not just in their literal creation over the eons of deep time through processes of deposition, erosion, freeze and thaw, floods, earthquakes, fires, continental drift, and seas rising and receding—but also in their metaphorical constructions. Land is mediated, made and unmade, valued and devalued through its interactions with humans and nonhumans, and our technologies and constructions, over and across generations. The most genuine attempts to capture and represent landscapes are also layered. Painted landscapes are built up from the flat of the canvas and the underpaint, deftly applied layers of pigment coming together to give a piece an arresting depth and dimension, a sense of fullness. Music meant to be representative of landscapes is similarly composed, constructed note upon note to try to capture in an auditory experience the feeling of being in a certain place, maybe even at a certain time.

The Appalachian landscape is compelling because of its layered nature too. It's framing as a place of endless, possibly dangerous, wildness inspired by the way each ridge, holler, and river turns and fades into another seemingly endlessly. The rocks that form the Blue Ridge Mountains, the crooked spine of the Appalachians and one of the oldest ranges on the planet, date to over one billion years ago and were thrust upward by the collision of tectonic plates over four hundred million years ago.[18] Left to sink and fold in and upon each other, they have been settling into their rolling layers ever since. Before the recession of the Laurentide ice sheet twenty thousand years ago, the region we know as Appalachia was a vast stretch of glacier, tundra, and from what is now called Tennessee southward were dense boreal oak-hickory and evergreen forests inhabited by diverse megafauna.[19] Humans have lived in viable settlements in the region for over twelve thousand years—possibly much longer.[20] To flatten this historically, geographically, ecologically, and culturally dense landscape into a wasteland of reductive "Trump country" narratives is an act of human, settler-colonial, white supremacy. When I go into the archive, when I sit down to write, I want to try to tell histories that feel as layered as this landscape they inhabit, and I think that this kind of historical writing is how we move beyond the damaging stereotypes of the region. So how do we get there?

Theory isn't the only thing that gives writing depth; you can tell a good story and never once touch a piece of theory. Compelling oral traditions and histories often come from marginalized folks with little access to literacy, let alone formal academic theory. But as a historian, certain theoretical literature and frames give me tools that allow me to tell these deeper stories. The theories I find most compelling are linked to the positional identities I approach my work from—maybe that seems obvious. But what makes the work of queer, Indigenous, and postcolonial scholars most compelling to me is the understanding that this work is intricately linked to fighting for the survival of our stories, our histories, and our knowledges. White cishetero supremacy in the academy would write these bodies of knowledge off as trendy, or in the extreme recent case of Critical Race Theory, dangerous and un-American.[21] But they give us the depth to tell good stories that colonial scholarship and extractive practices have only ever served to flatten.

Queering Appalachia is one of many ways I seek to return some of the layers to the flattened landscape. In thinking with queer lenses, I am able to see the dams and power grids of the TVA not just as static constructions but as systems wielded by the settler state engaged in their own processes of historical layering that erased as much as they created. The story that is often told of Appalachia isn't just violently wrong in its omissions and silences, it's boring. Its flatness is the hallmark of unimaginative settler-colonial constructions of landscapes as only value and capital to be extracted and of people to be controlled and reigned into specific ways of living aimed at creating a stable, profitable nation-state. It paints a picture, but it lacks the depth that makes a landscape come to life. This narrative is an act of dominance—not community, not construction—and it is representative of an admittedly powerful fraction of Appalachia, but never of the whole. Maybe no one story, or painting, or piece of music can truly capture the entirety of a landscape. Maybe instead of trying to capture wholes we craft our histories to tell smaller stories, parts of wholes, with care, about people and places we have meaningful connections to, and by weaving these smaller stories into one another we can build richer archives, deeper histories, better worlds, together.

NOTES

1   Akilah Johnson, "Boston. Racism. Image. Reality," *Boston Globe*, December 10, 2017, accessed October 10, 2021, https://apps.bostonglobe.com/spotlight/boston-racism-image-reality/series/image.

2   Maybe this is it?

3   This has become an increasingly important question in academic circles, as multiple revelations of false identity have come to light in the last year—the most recent about Dr. Jessica Krug at George Washington University, who built her career on her fabricated identification as an Afro-Latinx woman (she is a white Jewish woman from the Midwest). The regularity of "pretendian" identities has led Cherokee scholars to establish written guidelines about how they address identity claims—their full statement can be found at http://www.thinktsalagi.com. As a ᏣᎳᎩ ᎠᏰᎵ citizen I support this statement and always

welcome conversations with other Natives about my tribal status and proof of enrollment.

4   Hans Radder, "Why Technologies Are Inherently Normative," in *From Commodification to the Common Good: Reconstructing Science, Technology, and Society*, ed. Hans Radder (Pittsburgh: University of Pittsburgh Press, 2019) 45–87.

5   See, e.g., Anna Tsing, *Friction: An Ethnography of Global Connection* (Princeton, NJ: Princeton University Press, 2005); Penny Harvey and Hannah Knox, "The Enchantments of Infrastructure," *Mobilities* 7, no. 4 (November 2012): 521–36; Penny Harvey and Hannah Knox, *Roads: An Anthropology of Infrastructure and Expertise* (Ithaca, NY: Cornell University Press, 2015); Nikhil Anand, *Hydraulic City: Water and Infrastructures of Citizenship in Mumbai* (Durham, NC: Duke University Press, 2017); Brenda Chalfin, "'Wastelandia': Infrastructure and the Commonwealth of Waste in Urban Ghana," *Ethnos* 82, no. 4 (January 2016): 648–71.

6   The Allen plant was closed for operations in 2018, but the removal of several tons of toxic coal ash stored in unlined ponds on the property (and other, now closed TVA fossil plants as they transition to more renewable power sources) remains an ongoing issue that impacts low-income communities and communities of color throughout the South. For ongoing information about the fight against coal ash in Memphis, follow the community watchdog group Protect Our Aquifer at their website https://www.protectouraquifer.org or on Facebook.

7   Report: "Isolated Communities in Tennessee: A Preliminary Study," RG 142, Regional Studies and Surveys of the Social and Economics Div., Box 22, Folder: "Study: Isolated Communities in the Tennessee Valley," National Archives and Record Administration, Atlanta, Georgia; Paul Irvine, "Effect of Closed Schools on Adolescent Children," (Auburn, AL: Alabama Polytechnic Institute, 1934), RG 142, Regional Studies and Surveys of the Social and Economics Div., Box 29, Folder: "921 Schools (as an institution) A6 Effects of Closed Schools...," National Archives and Record Administration, Atlanta, Georgia; Map, "Place of Residence of Juvenile Court Cases-Roanoke 1924–1931," RG 142, Regional Studies and Surveys of the Social and Economics Div., Box 16, Folder: "Maps & General Information, Roanoke, VA," National Archives and Record Administration, Atlanta, Georgia.

8   A selection of these images are available online to view: National Archives at Atlanta, "Valley of the Dams: The Impact & Legacy of the Tennessee Valley Authority," accessed October 9, 2021, https://www.archives.gov/atlanta/exhibits/exhibits-tva.html.

9   Images 36, 37, and 38, RG 142, "Lewis Hine Photographs for the Tennessee Valley Authority, 1933–1933," various Box 1, Folder 1, National Archives and Record Administration, Atlanta, Georgia.

10   This is a reference to the first institutional history of the TVA; David E. Lilienthal, *TVA: Democracy on the March* (New York: Harper & Brothers, 1953).

11   Elizabeth Catte, *What You Are Getting Wrong about Appalachia* (Cleveland: Belt Publishing, 2018), 72.

12   Micah Cash, "Dangerous Waters," *Bitter Southerner*, accessed October 10, 2021, https://bittersoutherner.com/dangerous-waters-micah-cash#.X3JkjFlOlTY;

also see Marianne Leek, "When the TVA Came to Town," *Bitter Southerner*, accessed October 10, 2021, https://bittersoutherner.com/from-the-southern-perspective/when-the-tva-came-to-town; "Progress, Heartbreak, & Art: the TVA," *Bitter Southerner Podcast*, Season 2, Episode 7, accessed October 10, 2021, https://bittersoutherner.com/podcast/season-two-episode-seven.

13   For songs, see Jean Thomas, "The TVA Song"; Tessa Oglesby, "The Valley (TVA Song)"; Pete Seeger, "The TVA Song"; The Everybodyfields, "TVA"; Drive-By Truckers, "TVA" and "Uncle Frank"; Old Crow Medicine Show, "Half Mile Down"; for films, see *Wild River* (1960); *The Final Tide* (1990); *O Brother Where Art Thou* (2000); for ghost stories and giant fish tales, I recommend making a visit to, and chatting up locals at, any of the many manmade lakes that dot the greater southeast—Google works too.

14   Joel K. Bourne, "Coal's Other Dark Side," *National Geographic*, February 19, 2019, accessed October 10, 2021, https://www.nationalgeographic.com/environment/2019/02/coal-other-dark-side-toxic-ash.

15   Adam Denny, "A Drowning in the Foothills," in *Storytelling in Queer Appalachia: Imagining and Writing the Unspeakable Other*, ed. Hillery Glasy, Sherrie Gradin, and Rachael Ryerson (Morgantown: West Virginia University Press, 2020) 62–63.

16   J. Jack Halberstam, *In a Queer Place and Time: Transgender Bodies, Subcultural Lives* (New York: New York University Press, 2005).

17   Melissa Walker, "African Americans and TVA Reservoir Property Removal: Race in a New Deal Program," *Agricultural History* 72, no. 2 (Spring 1998): 417–28.

18   Richard P. Tollo, John N. Aleinikoff, Elizabeth A. Borduas, Alan P. Dickin, Robert H. McNutt, and C. Mark Fanning, "Grenvillian Magmatism in the Northern Virginia Blue Ridge: Petrologic Implications of Episodic Granitic Magma Production and the Significance of Postorogenic A-Type Charnockite," *Precambrian Research* 151, no. 3 (2006): 224–64.

19   Donald E. Davis, "Pleistocene: The Big Chill," in *Southern United States: An Environmental History*, ed. Donald E. Davis, Craig E. Colton, Megan Kate Nelson, Barbara L. Allen, and Mikko Saikku (Santa Barbara: ABC-CLIO, 2006) 1–2.

20   Davis et al., "Pleistocene," 11. The scientific debate over the arrival of human life to the Americas is still contested, with some recent evidence challenging the traditional "Bering Strait" theory of migration and positing that Indigenous peoples lived in what is now known as North and South American for significantly longer than scientists previously asserted. Oral native traditions have long challenged this scientific theory as well; see Carl Zimmer, "Humans Lived in North American 130,000 Years Ago, Study Claims," *New York Times*, April 26, 2017, accessed October 10, 2021, https://www.nytimes.com/2017/04/26/science/prehistoric-humans-north-america-california-nature-study.html; Alexander Ewen, "The Death of the Bering Strait Theory," *Indian Country Today*, August 12, 2016, accessed October 10, 2021, https://indiancountrytoday.com/archive/the-death-of-the-bering-strait-theory-cpHdFoIDpESCDCTpOe7q6w.

21   Matthew S. Schwartz, "Trump Tells Agencies to End Trainings on 'White Privilege' and 'Critical Race Theory,'" NPR, September 5, 2020, accessed October 10, 2021, https://tinyurl.com/kjzus49u.

ABOUT THE AUTHOR

Hannah Conway grew up in the rural farmlands just outside of Roanoke, Virginia, and is currently a PhD candidate in the History of Science department at Harvard University. They are a historian, anthropologist, and visual artist whose work examines infrastructural design, access, failure, environmental justice, and the intersections of artistic practice and science and technology studies. They hold MAs in History and the History of Science from the College of Charleston and Harvard University, as well as a BS in Technical Photography from Appalachian State University.

Index

Page numbers in *italic* refer to illustrations. "Passim" (literally "scattered") indicates intermittent discussion of a topic over a cluster of pages.

ABOUT PM PRESS

PM Press is an independent, radical publisher of books and media to educate, entertain, and inspire. Founded in 2007 by a small group of people with decades of publishing, media, and organizing experience, PM Press amplifies the voices of radical authors, artists, and activists. Our aim is to deliver bold political ideas and vital stories to all walks of life and arm the dreamers to demand the impossible. We have sold millions of copies of our books, most often one at a time, face to face. We're old enough to know what we're doing and young enough to know what's at stake. Join us to create a better world.

PM Press
PO Box 23912
Oakland, CA 94623
www.pmpress.org

PM Press in Europe
europe@pmpress.org
www.pmpress.org.uk

FRIENDS OF PM PRESS

These are indisputably momentous times—the financial system is melting down globally and the Empire is stumbling. Now more than ever there is a vital need for radical ideas.

In the years since its founding—and on a mere shoestring— PM Press has risen to the formidable challenge of publishing and distributing knowledge and entertainment for the struggles ahead. With over 450 releases to date, we have published an impressive and stimulating array of literature, art, music, politics, and culture. Using every available medium, we've succeeded in connecting those hungry for ideas and information to those putting them into practice.

Friends of PM allows you to directly help impact, amplify, and revitalize the discourse and actions of radical writers, filmmakers, and artists. It provides us with a stable foundation from which we can build upon our early successes and provides a much-needed subsidy for the materials that can't necessarily pay their own way. You can help make that happen—and receive every new title automatically delivered to your door once a month—by joining as a Friend of PM Press. And, we'll throw in a free T-shirt when you sign up.

Here are your options:

- **$30 a month** Get all books and pamphlets plus 50% discount on all webstore purchases

- **$40 a month** Get all PM Press releases (including CDs and DVDs) plus 50% discount on all webstore purchases

- **$100 a month** Superstar—Everything plus PM merchandise, free downloads, and 50% discount on all webstore purchases

For those who can't afford $30 or more a month, we have **Sustainer Rates** at $15, $10, and $5. Sustainers get a free PM Press T-shirt and a 50% discount on all purchases from our website.

Your Visa or Mastercard will be billed once a month, until you tell us to stop. Or until our efforts succeed in bringing the revolution around. Or the financial meltdown of Capital makes plastic redundant. Whichever comes first.

Bodies and Barriers: Queer Activists on Health

Adrian Shanker
with a Foreword by Rachel L. Levine, MD
and an Afterword by Kate Kendell

ISBN: 978-1-62963-784-6
$20.00   256 pages

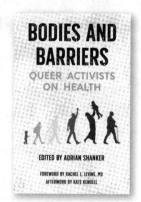

LGBT people pervasively experience health disparities, affecting every part of their bodies and lives. Yet many are still grappling to understand the mutually reinforcing health care challenges that lead to worsened health outcomes. *Bodies and Barriers* informs health care professionals, students in health professions, policymakers, and fellow activists about these challenges, providing insights and a road map for action that could improve queer health.

Through artfully articulated, data-informed essays by twenty-six well-known and emerging queer activists—including Alisa Bowman, Jack Harrison-Quintana, Liz Margolies, Robyn Ochs, Sean Strub, Justin Sabia-Tanis, Ryan Thoreson, Imani Woody, and more—*Bodies and Barriers* illuminates the health challenges LGBT people experience throughout their lives and challenges conventional wisdom about health care delivery. It probes deeply into the roots of the disparities faced by those in the LGBT community and provides crucial information to fight for health equity and better health outcomes.

The contributors to *Bodies and Barriers* look for tangible improvements, drawing from the history of HIV/AIDS in the U.S. and from struggles against health care bias and discrimination. At a galvanizing moment when LGBT people have experienced great strides in lived equality, but our health as a community still lags, here is an indispensable blueprint for change by some of the most passionate and important health activists in the LGBT movement today.

"*Now, more than ever, we need* Bodies and Barriers *to shine a spotlight on how and why good healthcare for LGBTQ people and our families is such a challenge.* Bodies and Barriers *provides a road map for all who are ready to fight for health equity—in the doctor's office, in the halls of government, or in the streets.*"
—Rea Carey, executive director, National LGBTQ Task Force

"Bodies and Barriers *helps LGBT community members understand the way people in the U.S. health services market erect barriers to anyone who is not the source of easy and immediate profit, and helps us all confront and break down these barriers. It helps families of LGBT people understand these obstacles and options for getting around them. And it helps health professionals hear the voices of all their patients, so that we learn to listen, and learn how to care for everyone.*"
—Michael Fine, MD, former director, Rhode Island Department of Health, author of *Health Care Revolt: How to Organize, Build a Health Care System, and Resuscitate Democracy All at the Same Time*

Queercore: How to Punk a Revolution: An Oral History

Edited by Liam Warfield, Walter Crasshole, and Yony Leyser with an Introduction by Anna Joy Springer and Lynn Breedlove

ISBN: 978-1-62963-796-9
$18.00   208 pages

Queercore: How to Punk a Revolution: An Oral History is the very first comprehensive overview of a movement that defied both the music underground and the LGBT mainstream community.

Through exclusive interviews with protagonists like Bruce LaBruce, G.B. Jones, Jayne County, Kathleen Hanna of Bikini Kill and Le Tigre, film director and author John Waters, Lynn Breedlove of Tribe 8, Jon Ginoli of Pansy Division, and many more, alongside a treasure trove of never-before-seen photographs and reprinted zines from the time, *Queercore* traces the history of a scene originally "fabricated" in the bedrooms and coffee shops of Toronto and San Francisco by a few young, queer punks to its emergence as a relevant and real revolution. *Queercore* is a down-to-details firsthand account of the movement explored by the people that lived it—from punk's early queer elements, to the moment that Toronto kids decided they needed to create a scene that didn't exist, to Pansy Division's infiltration of the mainstream, and the emergence of riot grrrl—as well as the clothes, zines, art, film, and music that made this movement an exciting middle finger to complacent gay and straight society. *Queercore* will stand as both a testament to radically gay politics and culture and an important reference for those who wish to better understand this explosive movement.

"*Finally, a book that centers on the wild, innovative, and fearless contributions queers made to punk rock, creating a punker-than-punk subculture beneath the subculture, Queercore. Gossipy and inspiring, a historical document and a call to arms during a time when the entire planet could use a dose of queer, creative rage.*"
—Michelle Tea, author of *Valencia*

"*I knew at an early age I didn't want to be part of a church, I wanted to be part of a circus. It's documents such as this book that give hope for our future. Anarchists, the queer community, the roots of punk, the Situationists, and all the other influential artistic guts eventually had to intersect. Queercore is completely logical, relevant, and badass.*"
—Justin Pearson, The Locust, Three One G

The Day the Klan Came to Town

Bill Campbell,
illustrated by Bizhan Khodabandeh
with Foreword by P. Djeli Clark

ISBN: 978-1-62963-872-0
$15.95   128 pages

The year is 1923. The Ku Klux Klan is at the height of its power in the US as membership swells into the millions and they expand beyond their original southern borders. As they continue their campaigns of terror against African Americans, their targets now also include Catholics and Jews, southern and eastern Europeans, all in the name of "white supremacy." Incorporating messages of moral decency, family values, and temperance, the Klan has slapped on a thin veneer of respectability and become a "civic organization," attracting new members, law enforcement, and politicians to their particular brand of white, Anglo-Saxon, and Protestant "Americanism."

Pennsylvania enthusiastically joined that wave. That was when the Grand Dragon of Pennsylvania decided to display the Klan's newfound power in a show of force. He chose a small town outside of Pittsburgh named after Andrew Carnegie, a small, unassuming borough full of Catholics and Jews, the perfect place to teach immigrants a "lesson." Some thirty thousand members of the Klan gathered from as far as Kentucky for "Karnegie Day." After initiating new members, they armed themselves with torches and guns to descend upon the town to show them exactly what Americanism was all about.

The Day the Klan Came to Town is a fictionalized retelling of the riot, focusing on a Sicilian immigrant, Primo Salerno. He is not a leader; he's a man with a troubled past. He was pulled from the sulfur mines of Sicily as a teen to fight in the First World War. Afterward, he became the focus of a local fascist and was forced to emigrate to the United States. He doesn't want to fight but feels that he may have no choice. The entire town needs him—and indeed everybody—to make a stand.

"A piece of American history in all its ugliness told as an astonishing coming together of misfits to stand up against a common threat. Bill brings an international scope to the history and a concise understanding of politics to the story. Bizhan's art is dazzling. This is a book for our times."
—Thi Bui, author of The Best We Could Do

"A fearless, brutal account of American history filtered through one town's relationship to immigration, identity, and 'othering.' The Day the Klan Came to Town lays history bare, making centuries-long connections to today. Vital."
—Nate Powell, illustrator of March

Black Metal Rainbows

Edited by Daniel Lukes & Stanimir Panayotov, designed by Jaci Raia

ISBN: 978-1-62963-881-2 (paperback)
978-1-62963-882-9 (hardcover)
$29.95/$59.95   400 pages

Black metal is a paradox. A noisy underground metal genre brimming with violence and virulence, it has captured the world's imagination for its harsh yet flamboyant style and infamous history involving arson, blasphemy, and murder. Today black metal is nothing less than a cultural battleground between those who claim it for nationalist and racist ends, and those who say: Nazi black metal fvck off!

Black Metal Rainbows is a radical collection of writers, artists, activists, and visionaries, including Drew Daniel, Kim Kelly, Laina Dawes, Espi Kvlt, Hunter Hunt-Hendrix, Svein Egil Hatlevik, Eugene S. Robinson, Margaret Killjoy, and many more. Across essays and theory-fictions, artworks and comics, we say out loud: Long live black metal's trve rainbow!

This unique volume envisions black metal as always already open, inclusive, and unlimited: a musical genre whose vital spirit of total antagonism rebels against the forces of political conservatism. Beyond its clichés of grimness, nihilism, reaction, and signature black/white corpse-paint sneer, black metal today is a vibrant and revolutionary paradigm. This book reveals its ludic, carnival worlds animated by spirits of joy and celebration, community and care, queerness and camp, LGBTQI+ identities and antifascist, antiracist, and left-wing politics, not to mention endless aesthetic experimentation and fabulousness. From the crypt to the cloud, Black Metal Rainbows unearths black metal's sparkling core and illuminates its prismatic spectrum: deep within the black, far beyond grimness, and over a darkly glittering rainbow!

"This is a manifesto as much as a book: A grand declaration of war against those who would confine black metal to crude invocations of masculine, heteronormative nativism. Black Metal Rainbows is an untamed collection of art, memoir, essays, and interviews that explode black metal into an infinity of kaleidoscopic pieces. It celebrates the truly unruly, the revolutionary and the playful, and it refuses to turn its subversive gaze away from black metal itself. A not-so-subtle reproach to those who condemn 'wokeness' as a pacification of black metal's vitality, Black Metal Rainbows demonstrates an awakening to black metal's true destiny."
—Keith Kahn-Harris, author of *Extreme Metal: Music and Culture on the Edge*

Crisis and Care: Queer Activist Responses to a Global Pandemic

Adrian Shanker
with a Foreword by Rea Carey

ISBN: 978-1-62963-935-2
$15.95   128 pages

Crisis and Care reveals what is possible when activists mobilize for the radical changes our society needs. In a time of great uncertainty, fear, and isolation, Queer activists organized for health equity, prison abolition, racial justice, and more. Nobody who lived through the COVID-19 pandemic will soon forget the challenges, sacrifices, and incredible loss felt during such an uncertain time in history. *Crisis and Care* anthologizes not what happened during COVID-19, or why it happened, but rather how Queer activists responded in real time. It considers the necessity to memorialize resiliency as well as loss, hope as well as pain, to remember the strides forward as well as the steps back. Activist contributors Zephyr Williams, Mark Travis Rivera, Jamie Gliksburg, Denise Spivak, Emmett Patterson, Omar Gonzales-Pagan, Kenyon Farrow, and more provide a radical lens through which future activists can consider effective strategies to make change, even or perhaps especially, during periods of crisis.

"Adrian Shanker has emerged in recent years as an urgent and prescient voice on matters concerning queer health. Crisis and Care: Queer Activist Responses to a Global Pandemic is timely, important and shares a message we ignore at our own peril. The response to COVID-19 from LGBTQ communities is informed by our own experience with a deadly pandemic made vastly worse by poor presidential leadership. Our lived experience over the past 40 years has valuable lessons for how we should be addressing today's viral threats."
—Sean Strub, author of *Body Counts: A Memoir of Politics, Sex, AIDS, and Survival*

"How did we respond? That is the central question in Crisis and Care. *Lots of books will look at COVID-19, but this book looks at how LGBTQ activists responded to one of the most challenging moments of our lives."*
—Igor Volsky, author of *Guns Down: How to Defeat the NRA and Build a Safer Future with Fewer Guns*

"In Crisis and Care, *Adrian Shanker and the contributing authors make the bold case that we are defined not by the bad things that happen in our society, but by how our community responds."*
—Robyn Ochs, editor of *Bi Women's Quarterly*